AWAKEN YOUR POWER WITHIN

Let Go of Fear
Discover Your Infinite Potential
Become Your True Self

Gerry Hussey

HACHETTE
BOOKS
IRELAND

First published in Ireland in 2021 by HACHETTE BOOKS IRELAND

1

Cataloguing in Publication Data is available from the British Library.

Quotation from 'Four Quartets' by T.S. Eliot used with permission of Faber and Faber Ltd

Trade paperback ISBN 9781529368888
Ebook ISBN 9781529368895
Audio ISBN 9781529368901

Typeset in Arno Pro by Bookends Publishing Services, Dublin
Printed and bound in Great Britain by Clays Ltd, Elcograf, S.p.A

Hachette Books Ireland policy is to use papers that are natural, renewable and recyclable products and made from wood grown in sustainable forests. The logging and manufacturing processes are expected to conform to the environmental regulations of the country of origin.

Hachette Books Ireland
8 Castlecourt Centre
Castleknock
Dublin 15, Ireland

A division of Hachette UK Ltd
Carmelite House, 50 Victoria Embankment, EC4Y 0DZ

www.hachettebooksireland.ie

Awaken Your Power Within

Gerry Hussey is a performance psychologist who has been working in the fields of health and performance for almost twenty years.

Through his programmes, keynote speaking engagements and events, Gerry helps clients strip away learned behaviours and thinking patterns to unclutter, clarify and overcome both internal and external obstacles and challenges, and ignite the best version of themselves from a mind, body and spirit perspective.

At the forefront of building high-performance teams and individuals, Gerry leads teams for success at high-profile competitions such as the Olympic Games, Heineken Cups, World Cups, and World and European championships. He also works with corporate organisations along with one-on-one sessions for individuals.

Gerry brings an unrivalled wealth of honesty, experience and infectious passion to everything he does. He has the ability to awaken, unlock and connect people and teams in a truly powerful manner.

Find Gerry at www.soulspace.ie or on Instagram @gerry_hussey or @soulspace_the_experience

For Miriam, Elijah, Dad and Mum

This book includes meditations, exercises and prompts for journalling. A pen and notebook might be useful to have nearby to record thoughts and revelations that come to you while reading.

Contents

PART 2: THE PATH TO YOUR TRUE SELF

Preface

This book is grounded in my own real-life experiences, my struggles and inner darkness. It shows exactly how my inner awakening of consciousness has enabled me to have experiences I never imagined, a peace I thought was not possible and love I never knew existed.

As a child, I had zero self-confidence, zero self-worth and I believed there was little good that could come of me. Today, I am a person who is able to share my lessons of self-confidence, self-worth, and the incredible beauty and possibility of life with elite athletes, global organisations and people all over the world.

Through changing my inner world, I have transformed my outer world – and, by doing this, I have manifested my childhood dreams.

We will start at my beginning so you can experience where my journey began, the path I have taken and what it has given me access to.

This book is written to document the extraordinary journey of a little boy who dared to ask bigger questions about himself and his place in the world, who dared to believe that there was something more to his life than struggle and suffering, and that there was something far more powerful and far more incredible than fear.

My hope is that it will help empower you to awaken from an unconscious sleepwalking through life and that it will assist you to shine a light on the unconscious self-limiting beliefs, habits, emotions and thinking patterns that you are holding on to and repeating.

This book will explore the powerful link between our thoughts and our emotions, and how they engage in our physical world. It will enable you to realise how much your current life is shaped by your past, and how freeing and liberating it is to break with that past and emerge into a new consciousness from which you can create a new present.

Many of us have experienced events that have caused us to feel really powerful emotions. These emotions could be positive or negative, but as long as the emotion of the past is stronger than the emotions we experience in the present, our minds, our thoughts and our experience of reality will still be locked within the stronger emotion of the past.

Fear, shame and guilt are usually the negative emotions we associate with past events and, unless we experience the more powerful feelings of love and gratitude in the present moment, we will always be locked into living within our past emotions. Unresolved relationship breakups, bereavements, business failures, family dynamics and traumas can all spark an emotional wave that we can find hard to break free from.

When we break out of these familiar past emotions, we are able to create a new future and we are no longer trapped in a predictable future where our tomorrow is simply an extension of our yesterday.

When we create a new and more powerful emotion, we also create a new and more powerful mindset – and, from this, we are able to create a new and more powerful future.

The book will also help you to realise how sacred and precious time is, and how short life is.

It will help you realise that many of us give away our precious time to things that do not make us happy and that do not help create the life we dream of – and can even take us away from it.

My hope is that this book will awaken in you a sense of how precious time is and make you question the things you give your time and energy to.

I will also explain the incredible and powerful connection between the mind and body, and how your thoughts and emotions directly impact your physical health. This book will provide an insight into the powerful fields of quantum physics, neuroscience and psychology, and how you must realise that your body, mind and spirit are actually one fully integrated system where each part is in constant communication with the others.

We are gaining a whole new understanding about the reality and the power of our non-physical dimensions, those parts of us that can't be seen – like passion, fun, laughter, love, fears, shame, guilt and energy. In fact, we are now learning that so much of our physical life is created from these non-physical dimensions.

We have never had a period in history where all these disciplines – psychology, neuroscience, gut health, quantum physics, traditional medicine – have come together in such a powerful way to deepen our understanding about the true nature of us human beings. When we combine these incredible disciplines, we are able to realise a whole new understanding of just how powerful the human mind and spirit are.

This book will show you how to gain a new clarity and insight into your life and, by asking better questions about what you really desire, will help you to understand what is actually important and, more importantly, who you really are.

Only when we can answer these questions about what we really want can we begin to plan and manifest a new life that is more closely aligned with our inner dreams and that reflects our truest and most powerful self.

This book will enable you to see that when you are willing to express yourself truly and live with passion and love, when you begin to release yourself from the unhealthy need for external approval – and the unhealthy oversensitivity to external criticism – a whole new life opens up. The very act of being able to look in the mirror and feel love and pride towards the person you see looking back is the single most transformative step you will ever take.

This book was written not just to enable you to heal but, equally importantly, to ensure you remain healthy and not wait until you get sick to begin to proactively mind and manage your health.

Parts of this book, and some of the concepts in it, may very well challenge you, and your current understanding and self-beliefs. There may even be a part of you that tries to resist the content and concepts in this book. It was the very same for me at the start.

When I began to discover some of these concepts and some of the science we will explore in this book, there was a part of me that didn't believe it and didn't want to believe it.

After a while, I realised these concepts were backed up by so much science that I had to acknowledge that my dis-beliefs were totally unfounded. I realised that it wasn't so much that I was resisting the concepts or the science, it was that part of me was actually resisting change, and resisting letting go of my suffering.

Sometimes, to get the answer we really need, or an answer we have never got, we have to go to a place we have never been, and open our minds to something we have never been open to before.

I hope you enjoy this journey. I hope you allow yourself to immerse your mind and open your heart fully to the potential within this book and the potential within you. I hope it will help you to realise and release all that is holding you back, and I hope it will waken your inner dreams and passions, and enable you to take the first and most powerful steps to self-affirmation, self-exploration and self-fulfilment.

The truth is that you are an infinite being with infinite potential, and all you need to do is waken to a new consciousness and a new vision of who you really are, and to the power that lies within you.

Trying to fill the inner void

Meet my eleven-year-old self

The alarm sounds and it feels much too early. The sun trickles through the curtain but I struggle to convince my eyes to accept the morning light. I struggle to gather the energy or the will to get out of bed and get dressed. Masses of thoughts and criticisms run through my mind. Like water released from the constraints of a dam, thoughts and emotions flood my system with incredible force, and I feel like I am drowning in them. Not only can I not see the bottom or the safe land, I can't even see the sea in which I'm drowning.

In automatic mode, my body makes its way to the bathroom and I freshen up, presenting an external picture that is very different to the one felt inside. It's even hard to feel the hot water of the shower on my skin against the avalanche of icy emotions inside.

Still in some type of automatic mode, my body makes its way into the kitchen, where I acknowledge my family with a mumble. At the breakfast table, I eat porridge but what I am really consuming is anger, anger at everyone at this table, anger at my own family – that I could be here, in so much pain, so

1

much distress, drowning before their eyes, and for them not even to notice, not even acknowledge my distress.

My cycle to school is my first chance to bring some type of order to these inner thoughts. It's my first chance where I have just enough energy to try to deal with them, my first chance to take on the army of demons that have been screaming for attention since the moment the alarm rang and gave them permission to attack.

I begin to create plans to support these thoughts. I began to make decisions about not speaking up in class because I knew it would reveal how stupid I was. Planning how I can avoid certain situations that may reveal the fact I have no friends, the excuses I would use when I'm not picked for the football team. I create plans to support all of these thoughts and beliefs. I have to – they control my life, and I believe, of course, that they are correct and are to be obeyed.

In the evening, I am back in bed. The countryside has become a vacuum of stillness, but my mind is still a torrent of noise. A distant howling dog expresses the need I have to scream, but I stay silent, fighting back tears. I want to scream at the sun not to go down, to stay up and keep me away from the terrors of the dark. The clock ticks and time moves on, but I stay the same, locked in a never-ending, frozen present of anger and fear. I imagine all the happy people going to bed, resting and closing their eyes, surrendering into a gentle sleep of happy dreams while I lie awake fighting demons.

If only I knew why my mind is like this, if only I knew why my brain is doing this and what is wrong with me. If only I knew how to stop it, but I don't.

I feel helpless.

There is nowhere I can run or hide from my own mind. It is this feeling of helplessness, this feeling of weakness that is the most painful. In an external world where there is nothing to be afraid of, I am terrified. In an external world where there is so much happiness, I am in a vacuum of relentless sadness.

Whatever is causing this, sleep is not the answer. I am too afraid to sleep, too afraid of what my mind might become and where it will go if I don't keep fighting it, trying to get it to stop. Staying awake isn't the answer either as I am exhausted.

What are the options?

Where else is there to go?

There is to be no peace or joy in either sleeping or waking. I can't carry this pain any longer, I can't bear this relentless cascade of fears and emotions. I can't carry this crushing feeling of being a failure any more – but where else is there to go? Where is it that pain and this crippling cascade of consciousness will ease? Where is it that this little boy can go because he simply can't take this pain any longer?

These are not easy questions to have to answer when you are eleven.

My name is Gerry. I was that little boy, lost and alone and contemplating suicide. This is where my story begins.

The destructive art of self-sabotage

Since as far back as I can remember, I had developed a way to live that enabled me to get through life, to survive. My life was about getting through each day and getting through each week. I was simply trying to hang in there and keep my head above the water, and yet I didn't even know what the water I was trying to keep above was.

I was living within the constraints and behaviours of my own self-limiting ways so I would not be exposed. I was avoiding all the things I dearly wanted to be part of for fear of being rejected. I was terrified that someone would see my inner fears – my anxious mind, my dark thoughts – and would think I was crazy or defective, so I hid them and avoided any situation where they might come to light.

I was so afraid of what people would think if they really knew what was going on in my mind. I was afraid that they would think I was weak for thinking like this. I was terrified of being exposed as the failure that I was.

I felt I had little choice but to live within the limits of my own fears and the limits of my own beliefs.

Back then, I didn't realise that both my fears and my beliefs could be changed. So, instead of changing my fears and my beliefs to suit the life I craved, I changed and constructed my life to fit within the limits of those fears and self-limiting beliefs.

All through my teenage years, I pushed everyone away, especially those who showed any interest in me or who wanted to be my friend and to get to know the real me. I kept everyone at a distance. I did this as an act of self-sabotage. As we will find out, self-sabotage is actually self-protection but,

> 'Back then, I didn't realise that both my fears and my beliefs could be changed.'

at this point, I knew little about it. At this point, I felt so much pain inside that I believed anyone who shared my life would be infected with the same pain. I believed that I would infect others with the same life-crushing negativity that pulsed through my heart and veins, and that waves of darkness would engulf those who came close to me – so I stayed away from everyone to protect them, to protect them from me.

My deepest inner belief was that I was weak. I was someone who couldn't even control his own mind. Someone who had failed to do this over and over, so I was a failure. I believed there was something intrinsically wrong with me. I thought that because I was so attached to so much sadness and anger, I might even be evil. Therefore, before anyone could find this out about me, I would push them away. I had perfected the art of self-sabotage, even if I couldn't label it as such.

At times, we all experience self-sabotage. We keep ourselves from meeting the perfect partner, we stop ourselves from going to our dream job, we inhibit ourselves from taking that leap of faith that would set our souls free. We all experience self-sabotage to some degree and I will explore why and how we can overcome this later in this book. But right then, and all through my teenage years, self-sabotage was my greatest friend, my ever-present coping mechanism, and I used it every single chance I got.

My fortress of isolation

My self-imposed, rejection-free cocoon was a fortress designed to protect me but, in fact, that fortress was actually the thing that kept me in isolation and loneliness, away from the people and things I loved and craved.

It was hard to see that at the time as I knew nothing about the power of the human mind. It was hard to understand that our thoughts are not reality and that our beliefs can be changed. It was far easier to stay in a world of self-perpetuating sadness, loneliness and pain, and just hope that it would go away – and even easier to stay in it and believe that it was all there was. I was living in a self-created bubble and it was like I was underwater all the time, unable to hear or see clearly, and all the time I was alone and gasping for air.

The truth about personality

Emotional and psychological pain can be like a thorn. However small, it can become infected if it is not removed. It becomes the locus of pain that will consume your attention, your thoughts and your emotions.

When combined, our attention, thoughts and emotions become our state of being – and if we stay in the same state of being for a sustained period, it becomes our personality. It becomes the state by which we come to know and recognise ourselves, the state we feel familiar with – and, in being familiar enough with it, we become familiar and comfortable with our own discomfort and we can actually become addicted to that state of being, that personality.

When we begin to believe that this is simply our personality – who we are – we believe that we have little choice about it, and so we must live within its limits as it is the way we are built or the way we are somehow prewired and that is set in stone forever.

To support and affirm this, we tell ourselves dysfunctional stories like: 'This is just the way I am' or 'That's my personality type' or 'I am a type A personality so that's just the way I think and act' or 'This is the way I have always been' – eventually, the worst of all dysfunctional stories, 'Sure it's too late to change now'. Very often what we describe as our personality is simply our emotional safe zone, a way of thinking, feeling and acting that has become so familiar, we feel safe and secure in it – our thinking, actions and behaviours become predictable to ourselves.

As we will find out in this book, the subconscious mind and the ego simply want the familiar, so we begin to believe in a personality box and we allow ourselves to get into this box and stay within it.

When we believe in a hardwired personality-type construct, we can spend our entire lives putting our energy into feeding and maintaining this constructed version of ourselves, stopping ourselves from being what we might become if we were willing to step out of the emotional safety zone we call a personality type and step into a whole new way of thinking, feeling and behaving. Sometimes we simply live within the limits of a personality type that we have actually created ourselves but were not born with. This doesn't mean that we don't have innate and natural tendencies and ways of being – of course we have, but we can expand, evolve and grow these any time we are willing to do the work required to create inner change.

> **'I didn't know back then that my personality was not set in stone and that I could actually change it.'**

I didn't know back then that my personality was not set in stone and that I could actually change it. So, I told myself that I just didn't have a very high intelligence, that I was very shy, that I was naturally a fearful person, that I wasn't a natural leader and that I was born with very low confidence. I told myself things that I would later prove were not true at all and I gave myself labels that I would go on to remove and prove incorrect.

At that time, I had a completely inaccurate belief about who I was and the abilities I had, but that is not surprising because, back then, I was buying into self-created labels and didn't know how to strip them away to reveal and become my true and authentic self. At that time in my life I had fallen into the it's-just-my-personality trap.

Putting up with the thorn became easier than removing it

We each carry different thorns. The feeling of not being seen or valued by a parent, of being rejected by friends, of being rejected by someone we gave our heart to. The fear of loving again, of spending our entire lives trying either to live up to or squeeze into the expectations of others, spending our lives trying to be what others want us to be.

Although the thorns can be different, the outcome is always the same – our lives are spent motivated by fear and not love. We chase other people's affirmation and never get our own. We live a life of playing small, suffocating our dreams and denying our brilliance in order to suit everyone else.

Eventually, the thorn you carry becomes so painful that you can no longer feel all the other parts of your body that are not infected, all you can feel is consuming pain. Psychological pain is the same. It becomes so much that all you can feel and focus on is the part of you – the part of your life – that is in pain, you feel nothing else and you lose sight of all your beautiful parts. All the good dissolves and disappears from your experience and your awareness of yourself, and you are left with a picture that contains only your failings and your pain.

We disguise our pain with maladaptive behaviours and socially acceptable addictions

The sad part of this is that so many of us can carry emotional or psychological pain for so long. We hide it, suppress it and distract ourselves from it, hoping it will go away, but really knowing it won't. We construct our whole lives, our behaviours and our dreams, to hide our thorns and hide our pains. This is maladaptive behaviour.

Sometimes, the loudest person in the room is the one trying to drown out their own inner pain. Sometimes, the person with the seven-day smile is the one trying to deflect you from their tears. Sometimes, the very motivated, very driven person is the one who is running away and afraid to sit still. Sometimes, the person who is addicted to adventure and

'Sometimes, the loudest person in the room is the one trying to drown out their own inner pain.'

extreme pursuits is the one looking to self-harm or self-punish. Very often, the people who drink too much and tell you they don't care about it are actually telling you they don't care about themselves.

Sport and business are two socially acceptable ways we can hide and disguise our pain. Obsession and self-harm can be described as 'drive' and 'fearlessness' – the inability to be happy with who you are right now drives you to want more medals and more promotions. Avoiding a dysfunctional family life drives you to spend far too long at the training ground or in the office, and an unhealthy need to be seen, to be loved, will drive you relentlessly to be the centre of attention and the person everyone is talking about.

We will use any behaviour or emotion we can to keep ourselves as the centre of attention, even if, at times, the behaviours and emotions we use are destructive to others or ourselves.

When pain turns to anger, we declare war on ourselves

When you carry this inner pain for long enough, it can simply become too much. Sadness, loneliness and despair give way, and all that is left is anger. Intense anger.

Even when I was a young boy, I became angry at my family, my teachers, my friends. Eventually, having been angry at everyone and anything external, I turned my anger inwards and declared war on myself. Anger turned to hate. Ferocious, sustained self-hate.

I hated myself for my mistakes.

I hated myself for the sad and lonely person I was.

I hated myself for all the things I wasn't achieving.

I hated myself because I wasn't the strong, confident person I wanted to be.

> 'I created a mask, a suit of armour, to hide my inner child and my inner weakness.'

I hated myself because, in my own eyes and through my own inner stories, I believed I was a failure.

I was none of the things I thought I should be.

I was none of the things I thought my parents wanted me to be.

I believed I was a failure and I had failed all those who loved me. I had betrayed them, something that could not go unpunished.

I needed to prove myself to everybody and anyone. I needed to prove my strength – I couldn't let the world see my delicate and hurting side. The only way to heal was to get angry and push through, to suppress and deny. I told myself to harden up, toughen up, get on with it. There was no place for weakness or silly sadness. Toughen up, bottle up, that's the only way to get through this. I marched on, wounded and sore, alone and drowning. I created a mask, a suit of armour, to hide my inner hurts, to keep my demons locked in and the outer world locked out.

We create masks to hide behind

Throughout my teenage years, I contemplated ending my life a number of times. I thought it was the only option. I had even thought in detail about how, when and where I could do it. It is a really bizarre situation to be in, and anyone who has experienced it will know that it is shocking how clear your mind can be in the midst of such thoughts. It's not that death is what you want – I don't know if anyone wants that – it's more that you're trying to ease the relentless pain, the non-stop thoughts and the ever-present feeling of being alone. It's almost like looking at life and the world from inside a soundless void, a vacuum, with a feeling that all of life and everything you wish for is on the other side of a glass wall but you can't get at it, you can't feel, sense or experience it.

I didn't want to die but I simply couldn't keep living, not this type of life.

In those dark days, I didn't know that I could change my life, that I could change my world simply by changing me. Therefore, I thought I was trapped into living this same reality, and that was something I couldn't bear to face.

Finding that one piece of me that was loveable

On one occasion, at the age of fifteen, as I prepared to end my life, I started to think about my mum. My incredible mum, who I love with all my heart. My incredible mum who I knew loved me even if I couldn't understand why. I love my mum dearly and I started to imagine what it would do to her if I went ahead and ended my life. This shook something inside me.

It was the first moment in my life where I actually allowed myself to look at evidence and realise that there was, in fact, someone who loved me.

Deep down, I knew, despite all my disguises, that my mum knew me, knew every part of me. If my mum was willing to love me, then, at some level, a piece of me must be loveable. For the briefest but most powerful of moments, I felt loved and I felt love. I began to realise that, as powerful as fear is – and it is powerful – there was something that was more powerful, more powerful than anxiety, more powerful than anger and more powerful than self-sabotage – and that is love. In that moment, I experienced love. As I allowed that feeling of love to flow through me without resisting it, I realised that I felt differently,

> 'I began to realise that, as powerful as fear is – and it is powerful – there was something more powerful, more powerful than anxiety, more powerful than anger and more powerful than self-sabotage – and that is love.'

mentally and physically. As I embraced the feeling of being loved and being loveable, everything in my being felt different, not just in my mind but in my body and, for that brief moment, I realised the true power of love and that how I feel emotionally has a massive impact on what I think and how I feel in my body.

For the first time that I could remember, it was like something clicked in my heart – a wave, a volt of electricity – and, when it did, for that split second, there was a whole new feeling. There was a curiosity over how my thoughts and physical sensations changed so fast in that moment of feeling loved and there was hope, hope that if my mind and body could change even for a brief moment, then maybe they could change forever.

I now started to wonder: *What if I could find and experience that piece of me? What if, even for a second, I could allow myself to see myself through my mum's eyes?* I became aware that I had something to fight for, and that maybe love was the starting point, maybe love was the medicine I needed, maybe love was the answer.

I decided I would give life another go and see if I could find and experience the part of me that my mum found loveable. The part of me in which love still existed and was still alive.

There was now something in me that wasn't quite ready to go, something that was still willing to believe that a different life was possible. There was still a part of me that was driven to stay, to live and to finally be able to experience the life, the freedom, the ease I had so desperately craved and had just experienced for the briefest of moments.

Chasing stuff

I was beginning the right journey but what I didn't know was that I was taking the wrong path.

The path I decided to take was to try to become the person who deserved my mother's love because, at that time, I wrongly believed that love was something we have to earn. I didn't realise that real love is choosing to love someone for who they are and not for what they do. So I set off to push, force and strive my way to becoming someone that was good enough, someone that deserved love.

I began to set goals around sport and school. I committed to doing everything I could to become somebody – somebody valuable, somebody people would like, someone my mother could be proud of. I wrote down all the things that I thought would make me a good son, all the things I needed to achieve to be considered valuable. I fell into the goal-and-target trap.

I began to believe that my self-worth was in the things I did, the things I won, the trophies, the titles, the exams, and not in the person I was.

I started chasing stuff.

For the next few years, I threw myself into the relentless and self-punishing pursuit of excellence, where I set higher and higher personal standards and goals that I desperately needed to live up to – all in a fraught desire to convince myself that I was different to my inner thoughts of worthlessness. This obsession with targets and winning became a non-stop need to win, where each win became a short-lived shift away from the belief that I was a lonely, terrified loser. But shortly after each win, the belief and the emotion of not being enough would reappear and the win would dissolve.

In competitive environments, obsession and desperation can easily be masked as focus, desire and determination. Self-punishment and self-harm can be masked as a willingness to break down and push through pain barriers. In highly competitive environments, I could hide my inability to accept who I was and replace it with a relentless desire to be someone else, chasing someone else's goals.

Winning was a temporary reprieve from the chaos of my mind, which was determined to rip itself apart. Each win in sport or school gave me a momentary feeling of happiness, while losing would further compound the feelings of uselessness and emptiness. I was changing my activities, and these new activities could temporarily change my emotion but, as soon as the pursuit stopped and the emotion dissolved, I realised that I was back to the same old belief. I didn't know then that unless I actually changed my innermost, deepest self-beliefs, I would always arrive back at the same place.

I came to fear losing, to the point where it was all I could think about. Of course, the more we fear something, the more energy we give it and the more we manifest it. I was so terrified of losing that I couldn't focus on anything else. I knew losing would bring about a tidal wave of self-fear and self-hate. It wasn't the actual losing, I feared the voice in my head that would be released if I lost, I feared the feeling in my heart, I feared being catapulted back into those moments when I first contemplated suicide as an eleven year old with no place to go, facing the abyss of nothingness.

It's who we are that matters, not what we do

Back then, I didn't realise that we should value ourselves for what we are, not for what we do or what we have. I didn't know that this focus on accepting the person we are – and coming to fully accept and love all parts of ourselves – is actually the first step in our transformation.

The biggest challenge most of us face is to accept ourselves fully as we are right now. To know that you are enough, that who you are right now is the perfect starting point from which you can create any future.

We spend far too long waiting for things before we start our transformation. We wait until our body shape changes ('When I lose a few pounds') or until we get the next promotion ('When I'll feel more successful') or we wait until we have more stuff, thinking that happiness can be found in the stuff. We wait for some external thing so that we can begin to feel like we're enough.

We forget that, very often, the things on the outside don't actually change how we feel on the inside.

The more we wait to become someone we can love, the more we are not loving the person we are. It means that the person we are right now has been judged and is rejected. If we keep sending that message to ourselves, it quickly forms our belief and, when we repeat this belief over and over, it becomes so powerful that we cannot break from it.

Even when we change things on the outside, change how we look, we will still remain the same on the inside. If we don't change our inner view of ourselves, then it doesn't matter what we change on the outside, we still face the same negative self-talk.

To love and accept yourself fully, exactly as you are right now, and to transform fear, anger and self-judgement into self-love and self-acceptance is the only place from which you can create a new future of ease and happiness. Back then, I didn't know any of this, so I set out to change everything on the outside in the hope that that would change everything on the inside.

I didn't know that no amount of external achievement or

> 'To love and accept yourself fully, exactly as you are right now, and to transform fear, anger and self-judgement into self-love and self-acceptance is the only place from which you can create a new future of ease and happiness.'

possessions can fill an internal hole. I kept filling my internal psychological hole with external physical things. I was in fact like someone trying to fill a bottomless bucket.

During this time, I constantly needed a new goal, a new win to keep the bucket of self-esteem from emptying. It was exhausting. When we need external wins, external validation and external material things to fill our internal hole, we are on a never-ending path. Eventually, if we are lucky, we realise no amount of external affirmation, no number of external wins, can overcome and erase an internal limiting belief.

We can all, at times, over-consume material things to fill an internal hole. We can work too hard, eat too much, consume too much alcohol, too much social media and even be too obsessed with fitness. We can all find something that gives us a momentary reprieve from the pain of loss or absence of inner peace, a momentary feeling of nourishment, but these are short-term and fleeting before we are quickly met with our own inner malnourishment – and instead of finally nourishing ourselves at this deeper level, we go to the quicker and more immediate solution of work, food, wine, chocolate or a pill.

But it's hard to know this when you are fifteen, so I pushed on. I bottled up and suppressed everything that was in my mind and in my heart in the hope that a medal in my hand would suddenly, somehow, bring the ease and peace I was so desperately craving. I was now on a relentless mission where I pushed myself constantly, further and further.

The revelation about dis-ease

Of course, when you push so hard there comes a time when you simply can't take any more. When you live with an inner lack of ease, it will eventually become a physical dis-ease. The revelation about the root cause of so much of our disease is right in front of us in the name – dis-ease simply means a lack of ease.

If you live with a high level of unease in your mind, it will eventually transfer chemically and physically into your body. I have come to realise that so much of our physical disease begins as a lack of ease in the mind or spirit, which I will explain in greater detail in Chapter 10 regarding the disease of distraction and the mind–body connection, but I didn't know any of this as a teenager, this was a revelation that I was about to get a sudden awakening to.

My internal dis-ease begins to appear in my physical body

Throughout my teenage years, I experienced physical symptoms, pains and headaches. I seemed to have a headache more often than not. I would get shooting pains that would run up and down my neck and I began to experience periods where my heart would race. At times, I thought I was having a heart attack.

Of course, at that time, I didn't know that the mind and body are actually connected, and that often the body is the blueprint or the physical

'I didn't know that, very often, the body is the tongue of the subconscious mind.'

manifestation of the mind. I didn't know that, very often, the body is the tongue of the subconscious mind. I didn't know that I started to get physical symptoms because of an emotional lack of ease.

I had certain physical symptoms, but we can all experience a range of symptoms or sensations and, if we listen to them in the right way, we may realise that they are actually messages and information about what is going on in our psychological and emotional world. They may not be pains at all – they may be more sensations or feelings of unease, dissatisfaction and worry, which can turn into anxiety.

If we ignore our psychological or emotional world long enough, then our incredible intelligent systems will switch the signal and the symptoms to the physical. If you ignore your mind long enough, it will eventually speak through your body and make sure you listen.

My parents took me to our GP, who said I was healthy, but I continued to get worse. More headaches, more racing heart, more physical signals, so they brought me to a consultant. This gave me so much hope, maybe I would finally get some answers about why I had always felt the way I did. Maybe this consultant, a professional who knows everything about health, would help me fix this pain and brokenness that I had lived with for so long.

I remember that day when, full of hope, we went to the consultant's office. I prayed he would see how much pain I was in and have the medicine to help me. He examined every part of my physical self. I sat in his office feeling like I couldn't breathe;

my heart was pumping so quickly that I, again, thought I was having a heart attack and I had a headache that felt like someone was shoving knives into my skull. Sitting there, in this turmoil, I watched as the doctor walked back into the room with a smile and said, 'Good news, all clear. He is a perfectly healthy young man.'

My heart sank. How could he say that? How could I be perfectly healthy and feel this terrible? What could explain the pounding in my head and in my heart? It made me feel so guilty about wasting my parents' time and money, and made me believe even more that I was weak.

'A perfectly healthy young man', was his expert opinion, so that is what we were to believe and accept. Nothing needs to change, everything is perfect. But, of course, I knew he had missed something, maybe he had missed everything.

He had never once asked me anything about my inner world – about the sleeplessness, the inner fear and anger, the loneliness and the self-hate. He simply ignored the terrified, lost boy sitting right in front of him and simply examined the physical. He missed everything that was right in front of him.

Exhausted and scared, I left his office and I had no idea what to do now or where to go; all I knew was that I was exhausted and unable to keep fighting, keep living the life I had been living. But I didn't know what else to do only push on, bottle up, toughen up, and stop wasting people's time.

The doctor's words kept coming back to me. I was 'perfectly healthy', there was nothing wrong with me, so I told myself

to stop complaining and get on with it. Eat healthily, exercise regularly, take care of the physical and all will be well – that's all it takes to be healthy, right? I had never even heard of a psychologist, no one had ever suggested I see one and no one had ever explained to me the mind–body connection. So, I focused only on the physical.

Our physical symptoms are simply a reflection of an emotional or psychological problem

The physical symptoms continued throughout my teenage years. At the age of twenty-three, things came to a head in what would prove to be a powerful catalyst and a period of incredible learning.

One day, after a training session, I started to feel very unwell. I was rushed to hospital and quickly admitted and treated for suspected pericarditis, which is an inflammation of the pericardium, the thin layers of a sac-like tissue that surround your heart and hold it in place. My heart was inflamed, enraged and constricted – which was also a perfect description of how my mind felt at that time.

The body gives us physical messages that tell us what is going on in the mind.

I thought, once again, that there was something wrong with me physically, because I had still not learned about the incredible mind–body connection. I had not learned that, often, our physical symptoms are simply a reflection of an emotional or psychological problem. So, I continued to try to fix the symptom and ignore the actual root cause.

I was hospitalised for a few weeks because the doctors were trying to get to the bottom of my condition. I was placed in a room where, over time, I would watch a number of my fellow patients pass away. For a period, I even believed I was next. I was so sick at that point, that I really thought I was nearing the end of my life.

The bizarre thing is that I had contemplated ending my life and now I thought the decision would be taken out of my hands. I didn't fear death – in fact, it seemed like a welcome reprieve – but during my time in hospital, I was forced to examine my life in a whole new way that would change everything.

Death is never the tragedy, realising at the end that you never actually lived your life is the tragedy

Slowly, my body began to recover. The pains began to ease and I stopped resisting and denying my situation. I stopped saying that someone had got it wrong, that I was too young and too healthy to be in this room, this room of old, sick people. Slowly, my anger towards my situation and towards everyone in the room turned to acceptance and then to curiosity. I finally had nowhere to go, nowhere to be, nothing to chase, no mask to hide behind and nothing to cling to. I was stripped bare, in nothing but a free pair of pyjamas from the hospital.

I began to get to know the five other men who I shared my hospital room with. We were different ages, with different backgrounds and different life stories. The room became our world. It was where we watched television together, listened to the radio and, at times, listened to each other as we shared our stories. As the days passed and we began to get to know each other more, we listened to the TV and radio less, and started to listen to each other more.

The freeing power of vulnerability

We were all trying our best to process and contemplate what was unfolding for each of us. As we gained each other's trust, we shared a little more about what was unfolding in each of our hearts.

During the day, we would sit and chat and joke about life and football. We would slag each other about where we were from and how the culchies were so lucky to be allowed to live in Dublin with the Jackeens. Even in the most distressing of environments, we found things to laugh about, temporarily anyway.

At night-time, we would lay in our beds, contemplating something a little deeper – the regrets for the things not pursued, how much time we had wasted on things that didn't matter, the meaning of life and the mystery of death that was clearly not far away from some of us. I never quite knew what each of the men was thinking as we lay silently in our beds at night-time, but the density of the silence was filled with a million questions, a million worries, fears and regrets, and a million images of people we loved and memories we clung to.

The silence was the most remarkable thing; at times none of us would speak a word, but the way we would catch each other's eye, the nod to a question not asked out loud, let me know that, in that silence, there was a powerful communication taking place.

As the time passed, we became closer. The stories we shared became deeper and more honest. As we were separated only by tiny, almost see-through, curtains, there was nowhere to hide physically, and I was beginning to realise there was nowhere to hide mentally or emotionally either.

As some of my room-mates got closer to the end of their lives, we began to see each other stripped bare, not just physically but mentally and emotionally. We began to see each other not by our age or accent or where we were from, but as terrified, remorseful, unsettled and lonely souls who were beginning to realise that, for some of us, there was no going back, no second chances, no more next years.

As our conversations deepened, I learned about the wives some of them had lost and how life seemed to have had such little meaning since their losses. I heard about the pain of having no relationship with a son and about the pain at having spent so many years separated from loved ones and maybe never getting the chance to change the vacuum that existed. In that little room, where six human beings were forced together, where six hearts were hurting physically and emotionally, and six souls were either worried about or preparing for death, I was receiving my greatest education.

It is amazing how well you can get to know somebody when you allow your outer mask to fall, when you are no longer afraid to bare your soul and speak your truth to each other. It is amazing how well you get to know somebody – and yourself – when you allow yourself to be vulnerable.

In that room, all six of us were forced to show our

vulnerabilities, our weaknesses and our fears, and, in doing so, we connected with each other on a level at which I had never connected with anyone up to that point. It forced me to drop the pretence, to drop my fear and my ego, and it allowed me to bare my soul completely – and I realised the freeing power of vulnerability.

In this short period, these men became my friends. They knew more about me than anyone else in the entire world, and their honesty and lack of bullshit enabled me to see myself in a whole new way. They became friends who listened to my inner, deepest fears and regrets, the people I could, for the first time in my life, be my true vulnerable self with and not be afraid of comparison or being judged. These men had no time or need for these things. It felt incredibly freeing to have this type of relationship in my life.

But, of course, we were all in that room for a reason. We were all sick in some way and some were dying. Over the course of my time there, I watched two of these new friends pass away. In the small room, with the almost see-through curtains, there wasn't much confidentiality. As each man passed away and said goodbye to his family, as each family experienced the fear and heartache of losing a loved one, I was there. I witnessed every tear and conversation and registered every regret.

In this little room, there was no getting away from the reality that was unfolding in front of me, there was no getting away from the reality of life. My running away from my fears was over and, for the first time, I had no distraction to run to, no mask to hide behind and no tomorrow to wait for; everything of importance in life was unfolding right there and it was both mind- and heart-blowing.

Slowly the room of six became a room of four. Then two others were transferred to another part of the hospital; I never saw them again and I don't know whatever happened to them.

That left two of us in the room. The conversations between us became quieter. As we waited for new arrivals to fill the empty beds, we tried to make sense of all that we had experienced, listened to and been part of in such a short period of time. Quickly, the empty beds began to fill with new people, new stories, new fears, new regrets and new unfolding vulnerability. But, this time, I didn't have the same interest in getting to know my room-mates. Perhaps it was because I was tired, or perhaps afraid that if I got to know them again, and hear their stories and form friendships, I would lose them too. There is only so much bereavement we can take in a short time and, at that moment, I'd had more than enough.

I still had my friend from the original six and we stuck together. We were now a two-man team and that was enough. We remembered the others for their jokes, their laughter and their stories, and, as best we could, we tried to keep their memories alive and fill the glaring emptiness as we waited for our own destinies to unfold.

❋

One morning, as I was having my breakfast, my friend's wife was visiting. As they chatted, a team of doctors walked into the room and pulled back the curtain around my friend's bed. I saw something on the doctors' faces as they walked in, I saw something in their eyes, and I knew the news was not good. As one doctor began to speak, I tried not to listen, but there was nowhere to go, nowhere to not witness what was being said.

Over the next few minutes, I heard one of the frankest, to-the-point and most factual conversations I had ever witnessed. The doctors had come to tell my friend that all of his test results were back, all the retests had been done and that, on data and evidence, their best advice was that he should go home to spend the little time he had left with his children.

I will never forget that conversation. It brought home to me how sacred and special time is, how valuable our health is and how we can simply never take anything or anyone for granted.

I remember him and his wife pleading with the doctors for some answer, some tiny shred of evidence that might suggest that this was not the truth, but every question they asked was met with the same answer, 'Spend as much time as you can with your family.'

We can put off so many things, we can be happy to wait, thinking – assuming, even – that we have more time than we actually have. The truth is that none of us knows exactly how much time we have or when that time will end.

The time to do anything of importance – to love, to hug, to kiss, to chase your dreams – is absolutely not in the future, it is now. That tiny room with the see-through curtains had become the place of my greatest education and I was finally beginning to hear the lessons.

Later that day, after he had packed his bags and was about to leave, he walked over to my bed to say goodbye. The tears were rolling down his face, yet he still found the kindness to wish me well and he said he would pray for me.

We went to shake each other's hand but instantly knew that that wasn't enough. We embraced each other in a hug that I will never forget. It was the first time in my life I had hugged a man. Until then, I thought that grown men didn't hug but there, in that moment, I knew that real men hug because love, kindness, compassion and support is neither a male nor female thing, these things are universal human traits and to be most human is to embrace all of them. It was the first time that I realised something else, too – I had never hugged my dad.

As we hugged, he said something really important to me. He told me to be sure to live life in the present, to take nothing or nobody for granted, to spend as much time with the people I love and to tell them every day that I love them. He told me to have fun and to remember that most of the things we worry about are never actually worth the worry.

I told him I would pray for him. I told him I hoped that everything would work out and that he would find peace. As his tears flowed, he slowly turned around and put his arms around his inconsolable wife, and together they walked out the door knowing they were about to face the greatest challenge of their lives.

I was overcome with anger, with fear and with sadness. I didn't know what to do, I just knew I wanted to cry, but I couldn't – for the first time in my life, I realised I had somehow lost, suppressed or buried my ability to cry. In this little room with see-through curtains, I was starting to understand myself with a clarity I had never experienced before.

For the next few days, I retreated into my own mind, into my own space, trying to contemplate and make sense of all that I was witnessing and experiencing. Over those days, I was so engaged in my own thoughts and emotions that even though I was aware that doctors were coming and going and sticking things into me and doing things to my body, I wasn't even interested. At that point, the most important thing for me to heal was my mind and my emotions.

I had realised that, very often, our pain and the source of our greatest sickness is actually in the non-physical part of our being, something that was an incredible awakening for me.

When we are faced with death, it's amazing what becomes instantly unimportant. These are usually the things we have spent so much of our lives, time and energy worrying about – the job we worked in, the boss we didn't like, the overtime we did that kept us away from loved ones, the holidays we said we couldn't afford, the exam we failed, the kitchen we didn't clean. All these things, and any importance we gave to them, evaporate instantly and we are left with an empty space, asking, 'What the hell was my life actually about? Why did I give so much time to those things?'

Coming this close to what I thought was the end and witnessing others go through the same made me ask some important questions, questions that I now believe we can all benefit from asking ourselves.

- What was my life about?
- Was there enough fun in my life?
- Was there enough laughter in my life?
- Did I spend enough time with the people I love?
- Did I tell them and show them I loved them?
- Was I open to being loved?
- Was I open to being loved as I was?
- Was I a good person who lived his values?
- What were my values?
- Was I kind to myself?
- Did I believe in myself?

In my case, there were a few more big questions that I needed to explore.

- Why did I never feel healthy?
- Why did I always feel that there was something wrong with me?
- What was I missing?
- What was everyone missing?
- If the answer wasn't in my physical body or my physical brain, then where was it?

These were important questions for me, and I would happily spend the rest of my life trying to answer them. That's the decision

I made as I fell asleep that night in the hospital all those years ago. *If I wake in the morning*, I thought, *if I survive this, I am committing to a life well lived.*

For the first time in my life, I had been stripped bare, my life and my beliefs about life were all exposed. At least I was beginning to get to the root of who I was and what my life was going to be about. I just needed a few more weeks of thinking and reflecting and reading to process all that had happened.

My experience in that hospital was that mental and emotional healing get very little or no time in general medical practice. While I was still in the middle of all of this experience – with my mind spinning, my emotions fluctuating, not knowing who I was anymore or where I was going or how I was going to make sense of everything – a doctor I had never met stood at the end of my bed. He read the charts for a couple of seconds and said, 'Mr Hussey, we are happy with your results. You are free to leave.'

I was released that afternoon having, again, been given a clean bill of health. While physically I was better and my symptoms had disappeared, I had no real explanation about why I had felt the way I had or what I could do to stop those feelings coming back. In some ways, I left the hospital no wiser than I went in – but maybe I left it a lot wiser and having learned everything I needed to learn.

You may think that being able to go home would have been amazing news. You would think that I would have been delighted to be told I was being released from hospital. After the fright of thinking I was dying, you would think that I would be delighted to be told I could leave, but I wasn't. I was terrified.

Terrified because I didn't know where to go or who I could speak to to help me process everything I had experienced or to help me find the answers I now needed. I was terrified of going back into my old life, I was terrified of falling back into the abyss of loneliness and emptiness that I had experienced before I went into hospital. Maybe I wasn't dying, but what I'd had up to that point hadn't felt like life, not a life I wanted to return to anyway.

The most incredible thing happened on the morning I was released. It was amazing how much I wanted to leave the hospital and, at the same time, how much I wanted to stay. I wasn't ready to go back to my old life. I wasn't ready to go back to the noise and distraction of the outside world. I wanted more time to try to process and understand, and I needed more time to heal mentally and emotionally. But, of course, I couldn't stay. Everyone expects you to be happy to be leaving the hospital, so I bottled up my emotions as I prepared to leave – packing away my fears along with my clothes into a small bag.

With a signature and the stroke of a pen, I was released. I walked out of the hospital and onto the busy city street, back into the hustle and bustle of everyday life, full of people rushing and racing. But something was different, something was very different – I was very different.

I now looked at the busy and distracted world through very different eyes. In my heart, I didn't want to go home to my parents' house because I didn't have the energy or know-how to share my stories, my feelings and my emotions with them. The truth is that I didn't know where to go. My old life wasn't home any more, the old me wasn't home any more. In the most fundamental way, I felt homeless.

I saw a little coffee shop on the other side of the street. I decided to go inside to collect myself and think about what to do next. I ordered a pot of tea but what I was buying was time. I needed to sit and think. As I sat there, my eyes and my heart began to well up, to the point where I could no longer hold back my tears, and I started to cry uncontrollably.

I didn't have the energy to worry about what other people thought of me, I didn't have the energy to get up and leave, so I sat there in the middle of a busy coffee shop, crying my eyes and my soul out. Noticing me, the waiter came over and left a number of napkins on my table. I could see by his face that he didn't know what to say. He obviously knew something was wrong. I realised how hard we can find it to say something when we see someone upset. I may have left the hospital, but I was still learning fast.

I used some of the napkins to wipe away my tears. As I sat and waited, the tears slowly began to subside; I began to catch my breath and regained a sense of calm. In that space of momentary calm, something flashed across my mind, a simple but powerful realisation that I would not be going back to my old life. I would no longer spend my life running away from myself, nor would I chase the things that other people wanted me to have or the things I thought I needed to have for other people to like me.

I realised that the time of running and racing was over, the time of constantly craving external distraction and external affirmation was over. My days of looking for and waiting for someone external to heal my pain was over. I realised that if I was going to have any life, any life of freedom and peace, I was going to have to first start living my own life, in my own way, where peace, love and happiness became the most important things.

I made the decision that I was no longer going to waste any of my precious time on things that didn't actually matter.

T.S. Eliot wrote a poem entitled 'Four Quartets'. In it, he has a powerful sentence that implies that, at the end of all our journeys, we will arrive back at the place of our beginning, but that we would know that place as if for the first time. I had read this poem thousands of times, but I had never really known what he was talking about. Now, for the first time in my life, it made perfect sense.

We are born naked and alone and we own nothing. We are born only with our personality, our inner dreams, our kindness, our compassion, and our ability to bring peace and love to ourselves and to others. At the end of our lives, we will again find ourselves in that place where we are naked and alone, where we have nothing but ourselves. The only thing that will matter on your final day is what you have found out about yourself and whether you are proud of the person you became – the things and people you prioritised, the love you shared, the dreams you pursued and the peace and presence you found in your life that enabled you to see and experience the magic of the universe.

On that day, depending on how you spent your life, the dreams you chased or buried and the love you embraced or hid from, you will be filled either with great pride or deep regret.

Now that I had experienced what a final day of life might feel like, I decided I would use that experience to live my life in a far more meaningful way, where I would get to experience and express myself more fully and understand everything that I was and everything that I could be.

There was no more waiting. The time to live was now.

I asked the waiter for a pen and, using the napkins that were left, I wrote down some simple but powerful things – promises to myself that have changed the course of my life. I promised myself that:

- I would stop running and I would value time more precisely.
- I would never take love for granted.
- I would be kinder to myself.
- I would stop worrying about what other people thought of me.
- I would value each and every day as a beautiful opportunity for me to understand and discover a little more about myself.

It sounds so simple, but the sentences I wrote on that little napkin have been the things that have enabled me to change the course of my life and manifest the things that I had dreamed about for years but which I never believed I deserved, let alone could achieve.

As I left that coffee shop, I was clear on one thing: my life was going to be about learning to love myself, to stop apologising for who I was and to stop comparing myself to others. I committed to using the precious time I had left to find a new, more loving relationship with myself, my family and my friends. I made myself a promise that when I came back to hospital for my last day, at whatever time or stage of my life that was, I would have no regrets.

I now realise that the old me, the old Gerry, did actually die that day. As I walked out of the coffee shop, I knew there was something new about me and my life, and I knew things would never be the same again.

I was now awakening my mind and spirit, and learning fast about their power and the internal power we all have to manifest and realise our dreams.

I followed my heart and took the brave decision that I would go to university to study psychology and philosophy. Not knowing if I was clever enough for it or not, I decided that I had to follow my heart as the subjects were ones that would enable me to explore and awaken to the questions I had burning inside.

It was also a brave decision because everyone told me that these were crazy subjects to pursue, and that it would be very hard to get a job with them. They told me to choose something more practical – but I was done with practical, I was done with trying to be good at things I had no interest in and I was beginning to develop my greatest gift, my ability to listen to my heart.

In my first philosophy lecture, our lecturer Dr Ann Power gave us an assignment for homework. I will never forget the title: 'What, in the last analysis, is everything?' How could she possibly expect me to know that?

At the end of the lecture, I plucked up the courage to ask her what the title meant, and she simply asked me what I thought it meant.

I said, 'I think you are asking us to tell you what life is about and what the universe is about.'

'That is exactly what I am asking you,' she replied.

Daunted by the size of the challenge and before I could filter my words, I asked, 'How am I meant to know that?'

In her incredible way, she simply replied, 'Well, tell me what your life is about and what the meaning of your universe is.'

In that split second, everything changed again. Philosophy is a subject where they say the question is often as important as the answer, and here, on my very first day, I had a question that I would spend the rest of my life answering.

What is my life about and what is the meaning of my universe?

For the first time, an educator was not firing external truths at me to remember, she was awakening my inner truths. I knew at that second that I was in the right place and that I had made the right decision about my subjects. This was far more important than getting a job, this was about getting meaning, getting an answer to who I was.

I would spend the next six years immersed in exploring new areas of study but always coming back to the same question: Who am I and what is the meaning of my universe?

It was a strange and unfamiliar path and, at times, I wondered if I was crazy. For those six years, I followed the same routine. During the day, I was busy in college studying psychology and philosophy and, in the evenings and weekends, I was reading, exploring and attending conferences in quantum physics, nutrition, and integrative health and wellness.

There were times when I was completely out of my depth and the easy thing would have been to walk away and leave it to the experts. But however limited my understanding of these subjects was – and is – they were opening up a whole new way of looking at and understanding myself. The first step to any breakthrough is getting yourself into the right space. Each discipline had a whole new language that I didn't speak or understand, but the truths and insights they gave me were worth the effort.

But there was a new ravenous curiosity in me, and even the little pieces from each field I could absorb were beginning to make perfect sense. It was like I was discovering an incredible jigsaw and each discipline had important pieces and I was beginning to put them together.

On finishing college, I couldn't wait to share my learnings and discoveries with the world or with anyone who would listen. I was beginning to realise what made me come alive: it was exploring the power of the human mind, the connection between the mind and the body, and the principle that we are 3D printers of energy and we have the ability to consciously create our own futures.

On leaving college, I knew I wanted to mix my two passions – sport and psychology – so creating a role as a sports psychologist was the next obvious step. To many people I knew, I was crazy to pursue such a profession, they thought my passion was a wasteful pursuit and that I would never make money or build a career. However, at this stage, I had spent long enough worrying about what other people thought, and living in the shadows of being afraid to pursue my own passions and dreams.

I was setting off on a whole new horizon, a whole new journey. I had the wind in my sails and passion in my soul.

I was a self-employed performance psychologist with little previous experience working with Olympic athletes, and yet the leaders of the Irish boxing team saw something in me and in my message that fascinated them, something they believed would help them transform their Olympic team. They took a risk on me.

I was assigned the role of the team mental-skills coach. Trusted to help high-performing athletes waken the power of their mind and to manifest their incredible dreams. Over a twelve-year period, I was fortunate to help guide that team through three Olympic Games, and European and world championships, winning multiple medals – in fact we won international gold medals at every weight category, at every level and at every age, to become the most successful team in the history of Irish sport.

These were transformative years and I learned so much about myself, my profession and the real power of human potential.

After years of living in the shadows of fear, I was finally stepping into the light of self-expression and I was awakening like never before.

Armed with an intense passion and my years of learning, I was on a mission to share my techniques with these high-performing boxers and quickly other Olympic sports came calling – track cycling, athletics, sailing, professional rugby. As a kid that grew up sports crazy, this was like a dream come true and I was now consciously awake and helping to awaken others who were passionate about exploring the power of the human mind and manifesting their dreams.

While many sports psychologists were speaking about arousal zones and goal setting, I was speaking about human spirit, spirituality, forgiveness, the power of love and finding pure consciousness. I was like a ship that had spent years tied and tangled up in the harbour and I had now finally rebuilt my vessel and hit the open seas with a hunger to learn, a relentless curiosity and a fearlessness that felt incredible.

Between 2008 and 2012, momentum grew. I started getting calls from some of the world's largest corporate brands asking if I would help them waken the minds of their employees and leaders, and help them ignite their inner potential.

By the age of thirty-two, I was the very proud owner of my own little business; I was my own boss with the freedom to follow my passion and I had a list of clients that included some of the most famous and most successful names in world sport and business. Twenty-one years after the first time I thought about taking my own life, I was helping others to save and change their own lives and to transform their dreams into reality.

Most importantly, I had left behind all beliefs that I was stupid. I wasn't clever in the traditional sense but I had found and ignited my own style of genius and that was good enough for me. I was excited by the people and things outside of me and I was at peace on the inside.

In the ten years since then, I have transferred my learnings solely from the world of sport to workshops and seminars all around the world. It's been a whole new departure where I left the safety of the sporting arena behind and backed myself to continue to follow my passion and pursue my dreams. Ships are safe in the harbour, but that is not what ships are built for.

Having spent years in inner darkness, there was finally a light that was burning bright inside me. It was a light that wasn't just my own, it was connected to a source outside of me that I still can't fully explain, but a source I believe and trust in with all my heart and soul. It was time for me to continue to ignite this inner light and, where possible, be a light for others that may have lost their own.

You might be surprised to think that that eleven-year-old boy could transform this much. There are times I am surprised too. There are times I have to catch myself and take a deep breath and take a moment to realise how far that eleven year old has come, how hard he has worked, and the courage he has had while on a journey that took him to and through the darkest places and also to places of incredible light and awakenings.

In what follows in this book, I will guide you through my real and honest journey with openness and insights and I will share with you powerful questions and facts about the nature of the human being and this universe, and then ask you questions that, if you are willing to answer, will liberate you to let go of fear and distraction and awaken your true self and manifest the life you dream about.

My name is Gerry. I am forty-two years old. I am a son, a brother, a husband, a dad – and I am at peace in a life beyond my dreams.

PART 1

The Power of Letting Go

Letting go of the physical-only understanding of my being

Because of my time in hospital, I came to believe that, if I was to find a solution to my health, to 'fix' my broken mind and my unlived life, it would not be found in a doctor's office where they look only at physical problems.

After a few more days of silence, reflection, exploring and awakening to the non-physical element of my life, I began to open my mind to the non-physical reality of the world.

I was realising that the illness I had been experiencing for so much of my life might have its root in non-physical aspects of my being. This prompted me to begin reading everything I could in order to learn more about our non-physical world, to try to understand myself and the reality of human health in a whole new way.

I made myself a promise, that I would open my mind to new realities and not allow scepticism to limit my pursuit of better health and deeper happiness.

I read books about the subjective nature of reality by seventeenth-century French philosopher René Descartes, who explained how each and every one of us can experience the same reality in totally different ways.

Descartes was aware that while he was experiencing the external world through his physical senses, there was also a part of him that was observing himself experiencing the world. He realised that there was a part of the human that is observing our physical dimension, and observing our thoughts and emotions.

Descartes was the first to make me realise two really important facts.

1. So much of how we experience the world is through our physical senses. Our senses can be wrong so we must apply a level of healthy questioning to our experiences and realise that so much of what we experience is actually a subjective construction. Therefore, we rarely see the world as it objectively is: we see it through the lens of our senses and our subjective reality.

2. Descartes' famous expression, 'I think, therefore I am' means that while he accepts his senses can be doubted, the fact that he is thinking and has awareness cannot be doubted. This work made me realise that our observer state is independent of the external physical world, and that it is this inner observer self that gives meaning and emotion

to the external world. The health and balance of our outer world therefore depends on the balance and health of our inner observer state.

My mind was opening up and my appetite for learning was increasing.

I discovered Einstein and his breakthrough realisation that everything in the universe begins as energy and, in fact, is at all times energy at its very core – that everything in the created world is connected by this energy, this invisible electrical field.

Through the work of Einstein and more modern quantum physicists, I began to realise there was a whole other dimension to our universe and to the human being that I had never known about or even considered. I realised that everything in the universe is energy, which meant that space, seemingly empty space, is not empty at all, but full of energy, full of vibrational frequency, full of information and pure potential waiting to be manifested by our minds. In fact, Einstein's work challenged me to begin to see that it is this energy, this vibrational frequency, that gives rise to all matter. Every single thing in this universe, at its very core, is energy and frequency, including us humans.

I discovered quantum physics and the study of the metaphysical and I suddenly realised that all these great minds, while using different languages, were all saying very similar things about creation and about life – about the vibrational frequency of the body, the power of the mind and how our thoughts and emotions impact our physical bodies and our physical world. I now realised that this independent inner self

'Your life and health are so much more than physical, your life and health are also emotional and spiritual.'

spoken about by Descartes is actually energy, and as energy it is free and infinite and has an incredible power to create. I just needed to learn how to direct and reshape what it was creating.

Your life and health are so much more than physical, your life and health are also emotional and spiritual, they are energy.

Yet despite the fact that all these great minds were saying that the non-physical, the energy, the frequency, and the spiritual all play a massive and central role in our health and happiness, in the hospital, the doctors seemed not to know anything about it or didn't view the non-physical aspect of health as a priority.

My time in hospital was a real eye-opener for me. Once again, the little room with see-through curtains became a place of learning and awakening, the place of my greatest education.

Beyond the physical

I had begun to realise that health was more than the absence of a physical ailment or injury, it had to be something to do with energy, vitality, optimism and maybe even happiness – and I had none of these things. If I was to finally begin to experience real health, beyond the absence of a physical ailment, then I needed to begin to first change my energy self.

I believed that some type of physical change or chemical substance would fix and heal me.

Albert Einstein said that the definition of insanity is

repeating the same process and expecting a different outcome. I decided I would take Einstein's advice and try something different. In my own limited way, I was now beginning to open up a whole new way of looking at and perceiving the world, a whole new way of looking at and perceiving myself.

The more I began to awaken to the non-physical reality of the world and myself, the more I experienced moments of insight into myself that gave me glimpses of hope and excitement that maybe now I was beginning to see where both my wounds and my healing lay, I was awakening to the power of my energy self.

Consciousness does not exist in the brain and doesn't even exist in the body

If I was to have a strong, healthy and connected body, then I would need to change my mind from one of negativity, disconnection and self-hurt to one of strong, healthy thoughts, thoughts that could both nourish and heal.

I needed to let go of and release myself from the cycle of negative thinking. It was now blatantly clear – in order to heal my body, I would need to heal my mind. I was learning that our brains are an important piece of our physical and chemical makeup, but our minds and emotions are not within the brain. Even today, neuroscience cannot prove that our thoughts and our awareness begin or exist in our brains.

For the first time, I could see that my pain, my sickness, my hurts were never in my physical brain and could never have been detected by doctors focusing on the physical world. My physical brain was working perfectly, but my mind was not.

My brain was responding to my mind, to my energy fields – just like a television. Sometimes, the picture on the television is blurred, it is jumbled, and what we experience is an annoying noise. Very often, the issue in this case has nothing to do with the physical television, it has to do with the signal quality that is feeding the television. We can try fixing the television all we want but, unless we fix the signal, it won't make the picture clear – unless we fix the signal, the television, although working perfectly, can only give us jumbled noise.

We can call the signal that feeds the brain, consciousness. Consciousness does not exist in the brain or anywhere else in the body. I explore states of consciousness more in Chapter 12 but have you ever asked yourself which part of you is responsible for fear, shame, guilt, regret, self-reflection or self-observation?

The astonishing thing is that there is not a single part of your physical anatomy that has the ability to feel emotion. Even your brain has no way of experiencing these emotions. Your neuro pathways, your synaptic connections, have no way of experiencing emotion. But we know that we as humans feel emotions and feel them powerfully – at times, these emotions that don't exist in the brain can actually override the logic of the brain. The human mind is far more powerful than the brain.

The mind is the part of you that is consciously observing you as you live your life. It is the part of you that makes you, you.

Many parts of the physical human being can be transplanted from one person to another and will work perfectly; but not the mind – the mind is a totally unique reality. It is your energy field and it gives rise to who you are, how you feel, and your state of being.

I was also discovering that my mind was not actually controlled by anyone or anything outside of me. It was controlled and maintained by me and me alone. I realised that, in many cases, it was my mind that was controlling and creating all that I experienced in my external, physical world.

I realised that it was my mind that was keeping me focused on and feeling the way I was feeling: and now I realised that my mind was changeable and I had the power to change it. It was me – the me that existed beyond any single part of my physical being.

Now that I was becoming aware of this part of me, I was beginning to understand that what made me was my personality, my passion and my energy. My inner dreams, my unique way of seeing the world, my interests and experiences were where the real me existed – and yet I had spent so long trying to strangle and suffocate those very parts of me. It was no wonder I suffered from tight chest and breathlessness so often when I was growing up. I was actually suffocating my own uniqueness and strangling my inner dreams.

It is important that we all ask ourselves from time to time which part of ourselves we are rejecting and suffocating and which part of our uniqueness we are strangling.

There were eight kids in my family, all physically similar, and regularly when we were meant to be in bed, we would be moving around out in the hall or sneaking into the kitchen for a late-night treat. My mum would be sitting watching TV with her back towards the kitchen, and without ever looking back to see who was there, she always knew who it was. I often wondered how she knew, how she could sense which of her eight children it was. When I asked, she would simply say, 'Of course I know. Ye are all different.'

The truth is we were, not just physically but energetically – and somehow my mum could pick up on our energy. For any mum or dad reading this, I know you know what I mean.

If anyone has ever entered a room or a house where there has been a bereavement, the minute you walk in the door, you feel it.

If anyone lives in a house with someone who suffers from anxiety or depression, the moment you come through the front door, before you even see that person, you can sense what mood they are in; you sense it, your energy field picks up theirs.

This is extremely important but is often overlooked or simply not explored. Each and every one of us has a distinct energy field and that energy field radiates and vibrates at a certain frequency that can be felt by others and even by ourselves when we open up to it. We are walking, talking energy fields, and it is your energy that makes you, you.

'Each and every one of us has a distinct energy field and that energy field radiates and vibrates at a certain frequency that can be felt by others and even by ourselves when we open up to it.'

I had a choice in where I was directing my mind and my energy. It was me who was rejecting who I was and comparing that person to who I thought I should be, it was me holding on to anger and frustration. I realised that we are not defined by the things and people we experience, we are defined by where we choose to put our energy.

TAKE A MOMENT

Each and every one of us is unique. We were born to stand out and be different, and yet we spend so much of our lives trying to fit in. We bend ourselves and our true personalities out of shape trying to fit in, trying to be accepted, and this can often mean that we dismiss and dismantle our authentic selves. We dismiss and supress our true self in the fear that it is not enough and, in doing so, we suppress our dreams, our passions, and we deny ourselves the life we deserve.

To better understand the internal belief systems that you hold about yourself, take a few minutes to sit down and answer the questions on the next two pages. Expand and elaborate where necessary so that you can really begin to gain clarity around your inner beliefs.

This journalling exercise may provide you with a greater level of awareness and understanding of some of the blockages that you may be holding internally in your life that could be reflecting externally in your physical world.

What are the beliefs you hold about yourself? Do you harbour more negative beliefs about yourself than positive ones?

1. Do you believe you are enough? If so, why? If not, why not?
2. Do you believe you are loved? Deeply loved and loveable? If so, why? If not, why not?
3. Do you believe you are worthy of the life that you dream of?
4. Do you believe you are brave, courageous and resilient?
5. Do you see your vulnerability as a sign of strength and power or as a sign of weakness?
6. Do you honour and truly cherish yourself in a kind, compassionate and loving way?
7. What are your personal and learned beliefs around money, prosperity and abundance?
8. Do you have a mindset that limits you?
9. Do you believe you are deserving?

What are the small daily changes that you would like to make:

•   in your life and lifestyle?
•   in your relationships – with yourself and others?
•   in your internal sense of self (e.g. confidence, belief, ease, joy, respect, love)?

Who and what is actually holding you back from making the changes you mentioned in this exercise?

_____

What would freeing yourself from these limiting beliefs look and feel like in your life?

Draw this picture or visualise it in your mind's eye. When you see this vision, how does it make you feel? What are the emotions that flood your heart?

_____

What is the first small step you can begin to take to release these limiting beliefs and make life-affirming changes in the direction of your dreams?

Write this step down _now_. Write it somewhere you can see it clearly every day. Share it with a friend or loved one. Say and sing it in your mind daily.

This is the beginning of your journey to greater peace and love.

2

Letting go of the fear
of not being enough

We can't outrun what's in our hearts

It is my belief that the single greatest emotional trauma a human being can experience is the feeling of being unloved or unlovable.

Through my studies and research, I was now realising that, for years, I was trapped chemically, psychologically, emotionally and energetically in trauma. My studies helped me to realise that any trauma can impact us on all these levels, and that, unless we heal that trauma in a multidimensional way, we will continue to infect the biology of our present self with the chemistry created by our past thoughts and emotions.

'The single greatest emotional trauma a human being can experience is the feeling of being unloved or unlovable.'

We will continue to flood the emotions and chemistry of our past through the body of the present.

When we hold trauma in our hearts and minds for long enough, it will eventually enter our bodies. I will explore trauma in greater detail in Chapter 3 and look at how we can release and heal from a multidimensional perspective,

'My studies helped me to realise that any trauma can impact us on all these levels, and that, unless we heal that trauma in a multidimensional way, we will continue to infect the biology of our present self with the chemistry created by our past thoughts and emotions.'

but, for now, I will focus on the importance of feeling unloved or unlovable, and highlight the impact that having this as an inner belief can have on us.

With this new awareness, I could now see what all the doctors who had examined me over the years had not been able to see. For the first time, I could see and feel the water I was drowning in, I could feel it in my heart and in every aspect of my being. It was emotional and psychological trauma that was causing my pain.

As Descartes said, many of our truths and perceptions are, at best, subjective constructs – so what we see and experience, what we know to be true about ourselves, may not be true to the outside world. This is where we have to own our own experience and identify our own truths. Deep in my heart, I felt unlovable and unloved. I felt unworthy of love, I felt a failure, I felt rejected, and this was my trauma that I needed to address.

All the love in the world from external sources could not change this feeling, as the feeling is caused not by the outside world but by my belief system. Until I opened my heart and my mind to the reality that I was, indeed, loveable, it did not matter how much love was poured on me from the outside, I would not allow myself to experience it. I would block it out and keep myself locked inside my own inner beliefs.

This awakening gave me the realisation that my illness wasn't imaginary, it wasn't made up, there wasn't something intrinsically wrong with me. I was simply trapped in unresolved emotional trauma caused by a belief that I was unlovable.

I could see the thing that kept me separate from the life and the love I desperately craved but was terrified of pursuing. I realised that before I could ever experience the love of another, before I could allow myself to be loved, I first had to address and overcome the self-created and self-imprisoning inner belief that I was unlovable. That started with me asking myself a few very simple questions: Can I even love myself? Can I see my own inner beauty? Can I begin to allow the healing and life-giving force of self-acceptance to finally flow through my heart and allow this self-created prison of ice to melt away?

We see the world not as it is but as we are

My parents were the best parents in the world. They worked incredibly hard and loved us with all their heart, but I didn't feel it – I felt unloved. I don't know why I created this inner story, I don't know why this fictional inner story became my compass.

It could have been something my dad said at some point that I internalised and took out of context. And then, the more I repeated it in my head, the more I added little bits to it to justify my inner beliefs.

Reflecting back on my younger life, I realised that I didn't have lots of demons in my mind, I had one and, it turned out, this demon wasn't the big scary monster I had imagined – it was my eight-year-old self. The small, gentle, broken child, broken with the belief that he was unlovable, was my demon.

> 'Reflecting back on my younger life, I realised that I didn't have lots of demons in my mind, I had one and, it turned out, this demon wasn't the big scary monster I had imagined – it was my eight-year-old self.'

Of course, my dad was never anything but an amazing and loving father to me but, in my eight-year-old mind, these were the stories I told myself. As I got older, I created a vision of the son I thought my dad deserved and would be able to love – and because I did not fit that fictional vision, I never imagined my dad could love me.

Many of us become imprisoned by our eight-year-old selves, and all the unresolved emotional needs and beliefs we had when we were eight years old. Of course, if we have a traumatic or high-emotional experience when we are older, this may override the emotional needs of our eight-year-old selves, and our most immediate healing may need to be at the age the experience or event happened. But eight years is a particularly significant point in our development.

From birth to eight, our brains are operating in what is known as theta waves. This brainwave pattern enables us to observe, process and learn new information, behaviours and beliefs very quickly – almost like downloading. However, it is an unfiltered type of downloading, where we don't have the capacity to really assess or analyse what we are receiving. So, we trust and believe what we see and what we feel.

My own life experience and my experience of working with clients has led me to believe that, as adults, many of us spend a lot of our lives trying to meet the unmet emotional needs that we had when we were eight years old. In my opinion, the beliefs we form about ourselves and the universe at the age of eight are often the beliefs about ourselves and the universe that we live and operate out of for the rest of our lives.

Revisiting and releasing your eight-year-old self

Before we go on to embrace our true selves, we must first let go of any belief system or emotional trauma that is holding us back.

Very often, I take my clients through a process that connects them and brings them face to face with their eight-year-old selves.

I get them to see, remember and re-experience what they were like when they were eight. I get them to describe what they looked like, how they felt, how loved or unloved they felt. I ask them if they felt in the shadow of brother or sister, or did they feel like they didn't fit in with friends.

I get them to express what beliefs they held about themselves at that age and what emotions they felt because of that belief. These are the thoughts, feelings and beliefs that were downloaded into their subconscious minds and that, unless they have consciously gone in and changed them, are still running in the background of their adult minds and still running their lives.

When you go back and revisit your eight-year-old self and

really understand the beliefs you held and the emotions you felt at that age, you will be amazed by how many of them are still the emotions and beliefs you are operating from today.

The way you allow people to treat you in adult relationships is how you believe you deserve to be treated, and this relates back to what you believed you deserved as a child.

TAKE A MOMENT

I think this is a really important exercise for all of us to do. To go back and reignite our baby self or inner child before we learned the habits of self-criticism and self-judgement, before we had a past to cling on to and a sense of self-doubt to hang over us. Going back to revisit and reignite our baby self is one of the most powerful things we can do. It was the starting point of my inner and outer transformation.

Close your eyes and see if you can remember a time in your childhood when you felt happy, content, joyful, safe perhaps.

What were you doing? Who was there? Can you see into the eyes of this little girl/boy and see their beauty? Can you see or feel their innocence, their delicacy, their purity? Can you begin to see the love in their eyes?

Close your eyes and see if you can remember a time in your childhood when you felt sad, lonely or upset. What were you doing? Who was with you? Can you see into the eyes of this little girl/boy and see their pain, sadness, loneliness or perhaps disappointment? Can you see their innocence, their delicacy, their purity? Can you begin to feel their deep desire to be seen, loved, appreciated, held and nurtured at this time?

When you look into the eyes of this little boy/girl, do you think they felt enough? Beautiful? Connected? Loved?

What do you think were the needs of this little child? Do you think they were met? Have these needs been met or resolved as your adult self?

You are this inner child. He/She still lives within you. This inner child may still be longing and yearning to be seen, loved, appreciated, held and nurtured. As an adult, you now have the ability, choice and permission to give this inner child your love. By simply being kind to yourself, cherishing your needs, honouring this beautiful, innocent little child within you – you can set him/her free and give them the permission and licence to finally feel they are enough.

Write a letter from your adult self to your eight-year-old self.

See the beauty and magnificence in this inner child. Can you give them back the feelings of joy that they once felt in their heart (like in your vision from the reflection just now)? Can you hold this inner child tightly and shower them with love when they are upset?

Can you tell them everything will be OK and that you see, hear and love them like you would any little child?

You are a beautiful part of this universe. Forgive yourself if you feel you need forgiving and let yourself be free of the pains, wounds and shames of the past. Look into your eyes with a gaze of empathy, compassion and love. Befriend your inner child (your inner self) and set yourself free. The choice is yours. Please choose wisely and honour your beautiful soul.

When I was eight, I never actually asked my dad if he loved me. I was too terrified to ask because I was so certain that his answer would be no – and it would have been just as crushing to hear it in real life as it was every time I said it to myself. I said it so many times in my mind that I forgot it was me who was saying it, and I actually began to believe that my dad must have said it at some point.

I was a prisoner of my own self-created story but also a prisoner of the fear of actually asking him.

It was simply my perception that I replayed over and over again, and it became my truth.

'A building cannot stand outside the size of its foundation, and our lives cannot be bigger than, better than or different from our inner beliefs.'

If you repeat something to yourself enough times, your mind will eventually believe it and, when you form a belief, it is very hard to have a life or an experience of life that is different to your deepest inner beliefs.

A building cannot stand outside the size of its foundation, and our lives cannot be bigger than, better than or different from our inner beliefs. Very often the limits of our world are simply the limits of our inner beliefs.

The way we can live within the limits of our self-created stories is amazing.

One of the most powerful skills I use all the time is to become aware of the stories that I am creating in my mind and to fact check them in the real world. When we start to separate fact from our inner narrative, we begin to let go of and break free from self-created and self-limiting narratives.

Because I had spent years building and creating this version of reality, I had fully bought into it. It is amazing how we can live in self-fulfilling ways that honour the beliefs we hold about ourselves and the world – even if honouring these beliefs leads us to self-limit or self-hurt. Very often the ego, which I will explain in Chapter 4, is more committed to experiencing the world in the way it expects to experience it and will manipulate every situation and opportunity to fit within its prior inner belief.

We often simply don't know when or where we pick up our

inner beliefs and stories. If we do, that's great because it gives us a real and tangible place from which we can explore, examine and reframe. But, even if we don't, the only questions we need to ask are: Are these inner stories and beliefs serving me well? Are they opening my mind and my heart or are they closing them? Are they founded on love or on fear?

And the final and most powerful question: Are these the stories I want to spend the rest of my life listening to and living from, or is it time to change the record?

We all have the ability to change the record and change our inner story and narrative.

I was realising the fact that we see the world not as it is but as we are.

We experience the world not as it actually is but through the lens of our inner beliefs and expectations. I know now that my outer world was just a place where things happened, I was the one who was interpreting those things through the lens of my own beliefs. It was me giving the external things meaning. I also realised that I was giving the same meaning to all external things despite the situations being different. It was me who was using everything in my outside world to affirm my inner stories and beliefs, and so keep me trapped in this feeling of loneliness.

My task now was to change this perception and thereby change my truth. Learning to accept and love ourselves fully as we are is the starting point of positive transformation that is founded on love and acceptance,

> 'We experience the world not as it actually is but through the lens of our inner beliefs and expectations.'

> 'Learning to accept and love ourselves fully as we are is the starting point of positive transformation that is founded on love and acceptance, and not fear and rejection.'

and not fear and rejection. Any transformation that has its origin and motivation in love and acceptance has a great chance of lasting, but any transformation founded on negative emotions – such as fear, anger or rejection – has little chance of creating a positive outcome.

Up to a point in my life, I could not accept who I was, I constantly told myself I wasn't good enough, not worthy, and the more I told myself this, the more my external world became an extension of those stories, words and beliefs.

I realised that my enemy, my demon, was nothing on the outside of me – it was not my dad, it was nothing in my past – my demon was my own thoughts about myself, my inability to know and accept my real self. In fact, my demon was not one that required aggression and strength to overcome, my demon was a terrified eight-year-old boy who needed only love.

I faced my biggest challenge to date: Could I love me for who I am and surrender the person I thought I needed to be or the person I thought my dad wanted me to be? The biggest question was: Could I love myself as I was?

The journey inwards

Throughout my twenties, I began slowly to listen to my inner self. I convinced myself to go on a retreat, a week-long silent retreat where there would be no external distractions, no noise or voices to drown out my inner voice.

Each day, we meditated to clear our minds and open our hearts. In other sessions, we simply used colours to paint our emotions. We created a life map, a timeline of our lives, and we drew ourselves at various points on that timeline – not only what we were like physically but also how we were emotionally, creating speech bubbles beside our drawings at each age to capture our self-talk patterns.

This was a revelation for me. I could see that, going back to my childhood, there was actually a time where I was happy and confident and full of fun. This exercise enabled me to see how I had changed along the way. I could really see myself from the outside and see the way my emotions changed, where my self-confidence disappeared and my self-critic appeared.

This was life-changing.

I could now spend time with each version of me, each evolution of me that existed at the different times of my life journey, and I could understand the specific causes and triggers that had influenced my inner pain. I could begin to reframe these situations with the benefit of hindsight and the benefit of an adult mind.

Eventually, I got to the point where I could meet each part of myself with kindness and compassion.

Of course my dad loved me. He loved me with all his heart. But I took things he said and did and manipulated them to suit my inner beliefs. That's what we do. Little things my dad said that might have meant nothing to someone else meant everything to me because I was looking for them to, I was looking for the part in everything that would confirm my inner beliefs.

> **'If I was the author of the stories that were causing my own unhappiness, could I write new, more powerful stories that would create my own happiness?'**

If we were working together and my dad got annoyed at the job we were doing, I would tell myself that he was annoyed with me. If he seemed tired, I didn't think that he might actually be tired from the incredible way he worked hard to provide for us, I would simply think he was tired of being with me. When I lost at sport, I would see his disappointment but didn't realise that he was disappointed *for* me. I told myself he was disappointed *in* me.

We see the world not as it is but as we are. We see the world through the lens of our inner beliefs.

This opened my mind to a new question: If I was the author of the stories that were causing my own unhappiness, could I write new, more powerful stories that would create my own happiness?

I realised our lives go in the direction of the stories we tell ourselves and I was committing to changing my inner stories and my inner dialogue. I was committing to turning my inner critic into my inner coach.

This is where I was introduced to the incredible work of Louise Hay and the power of self-affirmations.

Affirmations are the things we say both out loud and to ourselves that direct our thoughts and emotions, and that also send an energetic frequency to the outside world that, in turn, can manifest the things that we are thinking and affirming to ourselves.

The words we use create new neurological pathways in our

brains and new thinking habits. Our subconscious minds listen to everything we are saying externally and internally, so the more we say and repeat certain things, the more we affirm them as reality to our subconscious – and the more this happens, the more they become our subconscious beliefs.

We will explore the subconscious mind and how we create subconscious beliefs in greater detail in Chapter 12.

While most people don't believe they are actively doing affirmations, the truth is that every time we say or do something, that, in itself, is an affirmation. However, many of us are using negative affirmations without even realising it: 'I'm no good at that', 'That won't work out, things never work out for me', 'It's hard to meet someone special', 'I'm too busy', 'I don't have time'.

On the other hand, life affirmations are positive statements or beliefs that you say to yourself or read aloud on a daily basis. These affirmations are used to reprogramme our subconscious minds, to encourage us to believe certain things about ourselves or about the world and our place within it.

They are also used to help us manifest or create the reality we desire and to help us break old past limiting beliefs that no longer serve us.

By changing our thought process and our emotions, we are sending out a different frequency into the universe that will attract new and better outcomes that are in line with our new and better affirmations.

> 'While most people don't believe they are actively doing affirmations, the truth is that every time we say or do something, that, in itself, is an affirmation.'

Every day, I would listen to and repeat Louise Hay's self-affirmations over and over again until not only could I say them off by heart, but I could believe them in my heart. I was beginning to change my inner voice and I was beginning to change everything.

At this point, not only was I learning about the science of affirmations, I was absolutely experiencing the transformational power of them.

The work of Louise Hay became a constant part of my life – and it still is.

At first, I found it hard to repeat the self-affirming things she asked me to repeat, I was embarrassed saying them. Something in my psyche thought it was wrong to say affirming things about myself. Something in me thought it was wrong to use words like 'incredible' and 'inspirational' or 'special' and 'amazing' about myself. The very fact I thought it was wrong to even say these things revealed something deep in my being that needed to be addressed. First, I learned to say these words and, eventually, I began not only to say them but to believe them.

I had not only changed my inner and outer dialogue and narrative, I had also shaken up and begun to change my very deepest belief about who I was. I was beginning to give myself permission to believe in myself and my own brilliance, and I was beginning to give myself permission to let my own light shine brightly.

Louise Hay became an inspiration and I owe so much to the work and world she introduced me to. Although I never got to meet her, I believe I have met her successor, another inspirational woman who continues to awaken me to the same work, a woman with an equally incredible mind and way of understanding the science and emotional realities of the human being and this universe. Someone whose work will change our entire understanding of the power of the human mind and the human spirit.

I have not only met this woman, but I got to marry her, and every day she inspires me and awakens in me a greater insight into who I am and what we are all capable of. Her name is Miriam Hussey, and in this book I will share the meditations and self-reflection work she has created for me.

After listening to/reading books by Louise Hay, I began to take care of – and pride in – my new way of speaking and the things I was giving my energy to. I stopped saying self-limiting things and I began to create a whole new inner and outer dialogue.

When I allowed myself to be truthful to myself, I started to have more honest conversations and insights into myself. I began to see myself in a whole new way, unguarded and unmasked, and I began to see the reality of the little boy who desperately wanted to be loved but who had no idea that the only way he could ever feel truly loved was by learning first and foremost to love himself.

'I began to release all the expectations that I had placed on myself to be a certain type of person with a certain type of life. I stopped beating myself up for the things I wasn't, and I stopped comparing myself to the person I thought I should be.'

I began to release all the expectations that I had placed on myself to be a certain type of person with a certain type of life. I stopped beating myself up for the things I wasn't, and I stopped comparing myself to the person I thought I should be.

TAKE A MOMENT

Below are some examples of affirmations you can use:

- I am enough. I am loveable and I am loved.
- I am worthy, safe and secure. I choose to believe I am worthy. I choose to believe I matter.
- I show love and deep respect to my body and to my mind. I honour and cherish all parts of myself. I know I am enough.
- I am a divine spark of light. Capable of greatness. Deserving of love.
- I send love, compassion and healing energy to each and every cell in my body. I see my cells shining brightly and functioning beautifully. I choose to believe I am healthy and all is well.
- I can let go of my past. It is safe for me to do so. I now choose to release myself from past hurts or shame. I choose love. I choose forgiveness.
- A life of ease and grace is my divine birth right. I deserve to know peace. Deep within me lies an internal well of peace. An inner sanctuary that is truly divine. The natural resting place of my soul is peace.

- I release all shame of my body and what I think it should be. Today I will surrender to all that I am and I will drop into a place of inner peace through my life-force breath.

A simple but powerful transformational tool: a picture of your baby self

One of the most powerful things I did was to get a photograph of myself that had been taken on my first birthday. I was standing over my cake with the biggest smile ever and my eyes were opened wide with anticipation.

In the picture, I saw a beautiful little boy, full of excitement and deserving of all love. It took me a long time to fully accept that that beautiful boy was me. It took me a long time to realise that the beautiful little boy was still me and, somewhere inside me, he still craved love and laughter.

Every time I started to give out to myself, every time I started to be critical or judgemental of myself, I would stop and take that picture out. I would look into the eyes of that little boy and ask myself: Are you really going to speak like that to him?

This changed everything immediately. I was finally beginning to realise that, for years, I had been speaking to myself and treating myself in ways that I would never speak to anyone else. For years, I had allowed myself to say things about and to myself that were extremely negative, critical and destructive. If I had heard another person saying those things to someone else, I would have been appalled, and yet I was happy to sit and listen to my adult self saying these things to my inner baby self. Well, not anymore.

I decided I was going to stand up to myself for myself. I was going to learn to be kind and loving to my inner child, and I was going to make him know how special and loved he was. That moment, when I began to see myself as someone that deserved love and respect, was the moment everything changed.

I absolutely believe that so much of our pain in life is caused by the unhealthy relationship we have with our inner selves, and so much of our lives are spent trying to get an external item to fill an internal hole.

Until we can start to see ourselves as beautiful and loving beings who deserve love and respect, we are never going to have that love or that respect.

As already mentioned, a building cannot stand any bigger than the size of its foundations and your life cannot be any bigger or happier than the size of your inner beliefs. If you feel you deserve love and happiness, you will find ways to fulfil that belief. If you believe you deserve punishment and don't deserve true love, then you will fulfil that too.

Reigniting our greatest gift: the power of our pure human spirit

At our very core, before we learned different languages and different skills, before we learned to compare ourselves to others and before we learned fear or self-judgement, we all shared and connected with the same thing: human spirit.

Human spirit is by far the most powerful, most resilient,

most loving, most forgiving, most creative thing on this planet – and it has been given to each of us in full. You have had it since the day you were born. And the great news is that if your heart is still beating, then you still have it. This human spirit enables us to connect with those around us to form strong relationships based on love and vulnerability.

Your baby self

A baby captures your attention and transforms your emotions by its openness, its realness and its vulnerability. A baby doesn't try to be perfect or to look or speak in a certain way, it's simply too busy being real and being human. When we are at our most real and most human, we are also at our most beautiful and our most connected.

As babies, we learned to walk using nothing but the human spirit – no lifestyle guru, no fifteen-point strategy. We simply saw what we wanted, and we allowed the love of what we wanted to motivate and drive our actions. We placed the love of what we wanted above all else, including the fear of failure. We didn't wait for the perfect time, we simply let our hearts fill with the love of what we wanted. When love fills your heart, bravery quickly follows, and you had the bravery to stand up.

As we learned to walk, we fell – but we got back up. When we fell, we didn't give out to ourselves, we didn't worry about what other people thought of us and we didn't look for reasons to justify not trying again. We simply allowed the love of what we wanted to be more important than anything else. We continued to adapt and try new ways until we discovered the most important thing: balance. We discovered that balance is the starting point of everything.

We learned to take one step and then another and then another. We became so excited and so proud of each little step that we allowed that sense of pride and achievement to fuel and inspire the next step and, without even knowing it, we were up and running.

We often see babies walking about wearing only a nappy. They have zero concern about their body shape, they have zero care about clothes, they are simply too busy being happy and playing and discovering the universe.

With walking came new discoveries, things like mirrors. If you have ever witnessed a baby discover themselves for the first time, realise that the person looking back is actually themselves, you have witnessed something special. For hours, days and weeks, the baby will look in the mirror and connect with themselves.

If you have seen this, you will know it's a relationship based on excitement, wonder, amazement, curiosity, laughter and pride. So, before you go chasing the secret of wellness, ask yourself what it was that enabled your baby self to be so full of life, so resilient and to learn and adapt so quickly.

The same things that sustained you as a baby are the things that fuel and sustain our incredible human spirit:

1.   lots of sleep – eight to ten hours every night
2.   simple, wholesome food – and just enough of it.

Other things are also essential:

3.   a baby plays a lot – undirected fun and self-expression
4.   a baby laughs a lot – 200 or 300 times a day
5.   a baby feels deeply loved.

Have you lost some of these things since you became an adult?

Which of these five do you have in abundance? Which are you lacking? That's the answer right there.

Have you eaten or drunk something in the past few days that you wouldn't give to a baby? Are you getting enough sleep? Are you laughing and playing enough? Do you feel deeply loved?

Think of how a baby would develop if it was given good food and enough sleep but was deprived of play, laughter and love. Is that how you are developing?

Each and every one of us once looked in a mirror and saw wonder, excitement and pride. Is that what you see now? When was the last time you looked in the mirror and the only emotion you felt was pride and love? What and who changed that? What if the foundation block of wellness is actually the relationship you have with yourself?

Sometimes, it is the external voice of a parent or a teacher that we first hear saying something negative about us. We then internalise this voice and begin to repeat it over and over until it becomes our own inner voice and we become trapped in that story.

Sometimes, it may not be a voice but a situation or experience that made us feel a powerful emotion like fear, shame or guilt. Then, because these are such powerful emotions and cause us such inner pain, we avoid any potential situations where we may experience these emotions again. We spend our lives trying to avoid the recurrence of this pain and these emotions but the end result – spending our lives avoiding ourselves and avoiding our dreams – simply confirms our inner stories and emotions.

WHAT CAN YOU LEARN FROM YOUR BABY SELF? WHAT IGNITES YOUR POSITIVE GROWTH?

- You have human spirit in abundance.
- You have always had it, it's not something you have to earn or deserve, you either accept it or hide it.
- The human spirit is a powerful, motivating, compassionate thing capable of achieving incredible goals.
- It enables you to form powerful, connected, loving relationships by being present, real and vulnerable.
- By learning to walk, you proved that you are intrinsically motivated, resilient and adaptable when driven by the things you love.
- Fuelled by each little step, you turned your inner voice into your inner coach.

TAKE A MOMENT

Take some time to answer the following questions.

- Can you remember a time in your life when you didn't compare yourself with or judge yourself against those around you?
- Can you remember a time when you were carefree, fun and felt loved?
- Who was in your life at this time? Are they still in your life right now? Are you still spending time with these people or have you someone in your life that you can connect with on the same level right now?
- What were the things you did that brought these qualities into your life?
- Who has come into your life that has potentially taken some of them away from you?
- What experiences have you had that you think have taken these away from you?
- Can you identify three words that describe you as your baby self? Can you actively go after one of these qualities and bring it into your life today?

The beginning of my transformation

Rediscovering my baby self enabled me to realise some very important things about myself and about many human beings.

When I first arrived in this life, I did not know or experience loneliness, self-criticism or self-doubt. I didn't begin my life telling myself I wasn't good enough. Going back to my baby self and to a time before I learned about these self-defeating habits enabled me to gain the confidence to believe that there was nothing actually wrong with me. I realised that, with a little new learning, I could untangle my inner thinking and attachments and, by doing so, I could return to the bright-eyed and happy boy I once was.

This began an incredible process of healing and inner transformation. Rediscovering and reigniting my inner child made me realise something that was incredibly important. Looking at the picture of myself on my first birthday, standing to blow out my candle, my eyes full of laughter and my heart full of love, I realised that I wasn't born with some defect. I realised that, in fact, when I was born, I was perfectly happy, which meant my brain was more than capable of being happy and my heart was more than capable of being loved. In that picture, I did not see a child who felt scared and alone, I saw a child that was fearless and connected.

I realised that all of the things I thought were caused by a dysfunctional brain were, in fact, simply things that my perfectly healthy brain had learned and developed and perfected. It was almost like a skill that I had learned, a state of being that I had perfected. Now, for the first time, I realised that if I could learn it, I could unlearn it – or, at least, I could learn the skill and habit of peace and happiness I'd had when I was born.

If I was going to have a future, a happy future, a future of fun and laughter and inner peace, then maybe what I needed to do was go back to the beginning and remember

'It is important to remember that comparison, self-judgement and self-criticism are things that we learn, they are skills and thinking habits that we create within ourselves. If we can create these in the first place, then we can also learn new skills, such as self-compassion and non-comparison.'

who I was and what I was born with. When we are born, we are not born with fear or with comparison or self-criticism. We are born with curiosity, with self-expression, with a simple desire and openness to be loved and with an inner drive to grow, to express ourselves as we are.

It is important to remember that comparison, self-judgement and self-criticism are things that we learn, they are skills and thinking habits that we create within ourselves. If we can create these in the first place, then we can also learn new skills, such as self-compassion and non-comparison. We can create a whole new inner world that is free from self-judgement and self-criticism, an inner world that is more in alignment with the person we were born as and the person we are born to be.

3

Letting go of past traumas

I use a simple but powerful definition of trauma: 'Anything that overwhelms and overloads our central nervous system and causes it to become unbalanced, over-agitated and overactive.'

The things that overwhelm our central nervous system could be one big event or experience – such as losing a loved one, a relationship breakup, a health scare – or the accumulation of small stresses and setbacks – like failing exams, losing a job or any unresolved disappointment or reality that ignited fear in us.

When we encounter a situation or a life experience that is outside what we believed it would be, it triggers a sense of panic and uncertainty in our central nervous system, sending it into high alert and the fight-or-flight stress state.

Your mind has no way of knowing whether the threat is real in the world or simply imagined but, as long as you are thinking about it – remembering and replaying the trauma, or even anticipating trauma – that very act of thinking about it, of attaching your thoughts and energy to it, means your body will not only believe that it is real but will believe that it is happening right here, right now.

Unless you take time to fully heal the trauma and release it from your body, mind and energy, your central nervous system will keep responding to it over and over again. It will keep you locked in a frozen state of being that may very well have nothing to do with the reality of your current external world, but with a memory or expectation.

If you have had any such trauma in your past, if you had things or situations that overwhelmed you, that at one time overwhelmed your central nervous system, if you had things or situations that caused elevated emotions that you have not yet digested and resolved, then it is quite possible that your mind and nervous system are still trapped in the response to that trauma.

Your emotions and thoughts fire specific pathways in your brain. Each time you fire these pathways, your brain doesn't know if the experience is happening again or if you are simply remembering it. Your brain won't take a chance, so it presumes that the trauma is happening again and it creates all the same physical, mental, emotional, chemical and physiological responses as the original incident. You are therefore re-experiencing the trauma over and over again, as if it is happening again.

The power of your thoughts makes the trauma present in your life, so now the trauma is not actually in your past, and you are living in the middle of it unable to move on or to think or feel

'Releasing unresolved trauma and undigested emotions is one of the most important journeys and tasks you will ever undertake, and it is also the most powerful and freeing.'

life outside of it. This is the state of the 'frozen present' and, as long as you are trapped and imprisoned in it, your thinking and happiness can be no different than they were at the time of the trauma.

Releasing unresolved trauma and undigested emotions is one of the most important journeys and tasks you will ever undertake, and it is also the most powerful and freeing. Ultimately, it is the only one that will enable you to finally step out of the past and into the present as it is only from the place of the 'new present' that you can begin to create and manifest your new future.

Fear, shame and guilt. These are the most destructive emotions that you can experience.

Up to a point in my life, I had this constant undercurrent of anxiety running through my mind and my inner world. I found it hard to be still, hard to slow down and hard to be alone with myself. I passed it off by telling myself I was just 'high energy' or that it was just my personality type but, deep down, I knew it didn't feel right. How could it be my personality when it didn't feel right to me?

Back then, I didn't know anything about how trauma activates the central nervous system. I didn't know that, very often, anxiety is simply an overwhelmed central nervous system. I didn't realise then that anxiety was very often a very natural and healthy response to an unresolved trauma or an unresolved fear. I simply thought that anxiety meant there was something wrong with me, that it was a sign of a defective mind, a defective system. I didn't realise then that it was actually the sign of a very healthy, well-functioning but simply overwhelmed central nervous system that was out of balance from years of negative self-talk, rejection of self and a relentless need to push myself far too hard.

I had a decision to make: Was this the way I wanted to spend the rest of my life? Running from my mind, looking to the outside world for healing, and rejecting my soul and dismissing my very personality? A life of rejecting and despising who I believed I was simply because I wasn't the person I believed I should be, the fictional character that I had created in my mind? The answer was no, a clear and powerful no. I was tired of running, I was tired of never sitting still, I was tired of hating the person I met when I was alone. If I was to have any life worth living, a life of ease and peace, I needed to address and release my trauma.

As I came to this awakening, I also realised that I may not have to wait for an external expert or medication to remove my anxiety. I realised that one of the greatest creations on the planet – and perhaps the greatest pharmacy on the planet – is, in fact, our central nervous system and that I actually had the power and ability to rebalance it.

Your central nervous system isn't some kind of foreign or mechanical system that controls you. Your central nervous system is part of you, it is you.

It's not actually an independent system that does what it likes, it is actually connected to all of you: your thoughts, your emotions, your self-talk, the things you think about, the memories you replay and the stories you tell yourself. I was realising that our central nervous system is not always responding to the things that happen outside of ourselves but is often simply responding to our thoughts, beliefs, emotions and the meaning we give to the things that happen outside of us.

Just because your central nervous system is overloaded or overactive doesn't always mean there is something intrinsically or biologically or chemically wrong with it; very often there is absolutely nothing wrong with it, it is simply a physical manifestation of your unresolved emotions, fears and traumas.

It was time for me to really commit to rebalancing my central nervous system, and the good news is that it was a lot simpler than I thought – it involved breathing, recovery and rest, self-talk, healthier food, and moving.

As I began to experience the power of being able to slow my central nervous system, the benefits of understanding that it was me who controls it and not my central nervous system that controls me became clear.

I started to experience moments of inner calm, moments of inner peace, and moments when I was still and listened to my inner world. I heard something amazing, something I couldn't remember hearing before. It was the most liberating sound I had ever heard, or at least remembered hearing – the sound of silence, the sound of calm, the sound of inner peace. For a boy who had only known a constant cascade of thoughts and inner noise that deafened and drowned me, my new inner silence was incredible.

The new breathing techniques and routines, the new self-talk patterns, the new food changes were all working, and I could feel the difference, but there were still more decisions I needed to make, and deeper healing that I needed to do.

I decided that the days of running, of constantly needing distraction, external approval and external affirmation, were over. I realised that if my life was to change for the better and for the long term, I simply couldn't go back to my old ways of living.

Letting go of the belief that your past has to shape your future

The reality for many of us is that our minds get caught up with or fixated on the same thoughts, the same beliefs, the same chemical reality and the same way of being. We get stuck replaying the same reality over and over again, experiencing the same situations again and again, and living within the same limits all the time. We become frozen entities in a flowing universe.

Every single thing in your world is in a constant process of change, nothing stays the same. Trees, clouds, oceans are constantly changing and moving. Every single cell in your body is renewing and changing all the time – your hair is growing, your nails are growing, your food is digesting, your blood is being oxygenated. Everything in your physical and physiological world is constantly changing – except, possibly, your thinking and your mind. You can

> 'We become frozen entities in a flowing universe.'

become stagnated in your own life, your body and your mind unless you choose to let go of your past.

What we don't repair, we repeat

I have learned beyond doubt that if we don't begin to recognise where our mind and beliefs are fixated, if we don't learn how to change and reshape our thinking, our future will simply be a repeat of our past. I believe that what we don't repair, we repeat.

What I have become absolutely certain of, both in my own lived experience and in the work I do with countless clients, is that our future does not have to be defined by our past. Regardless of the past that we've had, regardless of the things that have happened to us, we all get to choose which parts of our past we take into the future and which parts we let go and leave behind.

The person you were in the past has absolutely no bearing on the person you can be in the future. The way you thought in the past, the way you felt in the past, the things you did in the past have no bearing on your future, if you decide that you no longer wish to carry them and relive them.

There is a gift that each of us possesses – the ability to reshape and recreate our inner personality. Every single one of us has the ability to reshape how our brains think. Each one of us has the ability to reshape and reprogramme our subconscious beliefs, programmes and expectations.

Each one of us has the ability to look into our past and ask three simple questions: Which parts of my past am I holding on to? Which parts of my past am I being defined by? Which parts of my past am I replaying over and over in my mind?

We now know that when we replay an event or a thought in our minds, we also replay it and make it present in our bodies and our emotional energy fields.

We can choose to let go of all the old ways of thinking and feeling. We can resolve and dissolve old experiences and allow them to be replaced by new, more powerful ones. For some people who have experienced deep trauma, that can be very challenging and can take work, but it is possible to dissolve and resolve it. When a trauma runs so deep, it can of course colour and influence everything in our life for a period, and it can take sustained work to heal. However, we need to know that experiencing trauma is very natural, but staying within that trauma forever is not natural. Human beings can and do resolve and reframe even the deepest trauma, and find a way to begin to live again with ease, passion and laughter.

Each one of us has a simple choice to make. You can be defined by your past or you can break up with your past, break up with old ways of thinking – old events that happened to you, old things that were said to you or about you. You can choose to let all of the old ways and experiences resolve and dissolve and be replaced by the new.

You can even break up with the person and personality you used to be. You can break up with the outdated beliefs that you hold. By changing your thinking, by changing how you

'By changing your thinking, by changing how you feel and how you believe, you begin to change everything.'

feel and how you believe, you begin to change everything. The things you have done and the things that have happened to you have absolutely no need or power to define you in the future. You – and only you – must define what you and your future will look and feel like, and only you must decide which parts of your future will be made up from the things from your past.

At various times in your life, you need to give yourself the gift of breaking up with yourself and breaking up with your own identity and your own stories and inner beliefs. When you do, when you change your personality, you change everything in your outer reality.

Letting go of the things we cling to that keep us locked in the past

Imagine a person in the sea in the middle of nowhere, clinging to a log. That person will spend the next number of hours praying to be rescued, but, while they cling to the log, their mind is noticing that the log is keeping them safe. They are becoming not just physically attached to the log, but emotionally and energetically attached too.

Despite consciously praying for someone to help, the most amazing thing happens when the rescue helicopter eventually arrives. When the rescue pilots lower the basket, they will stop just a metre or two over the person that is desperately clinging to the log and prepare to begin the rescue. After hours or days praying for the helicopter to rescue them, it is actually happening. The most remarkable thing is that the biggest challenge the rescue team have appears at the very start of the rescue when they ask the person to let go of the log and reach up to them. The rescuers hear the same thing again and again: when they ask the person to let go of the log, their response is always, 'I can't let go.'

Most people, at that moment, can't let go of the log. The log has been the thing that has kept them safe, it has kept them alive. In some ways, the log becomes part of their safety and their identity.

Think of the trauma, the hurtful event in your past, as the log that your ego clings to for identity and self-expression. If there is trauma in your past, it can become so much a part of your story and your identity, that it can become terrifying to let it go.

The starting point is creating a vison of yourself and your future that is so inspiring and powerful that it ignites a new emotion of hope and excitement. So your mind will be drawn towards this new, exciting vision of the future – and, in order to attach itself to this vision of the future, it will release itself from the past. Giving yourself permission to create a future vision that inspires and excites you, a future vison that is free from the suffering of the past, is so important.

There came a day in my own life when I had to consciously choose to stop going back into my past, stop using my past to justify my present situation and define my future. There came a time when I had to make peace with my past, make peace with my past darkness and past situations, and remove my emotional attachment from them.

To do this I went to counselling – shortly after I was released from hospital, and had committed to giving myself a chance at living a new life. I knew that in order for me to embrace the new, I had to release the old.

It was a daunting task, where I bared my soul to a stranger. Session after session, I would sit with my counsellor and share my inner thoughts and emotions, share my hurts and my fears. Leslie Shoemaker, the woman I went to, was incredible. A very warm and friendly person who made me feel at ease, but tough enough that she didn't allow me to indulge in my own excuses any more. I knew she was committed to one thing – helping me to find inner peace, the one thing I craved.

Our conversations would flow and stop, I would open up and shut down, I would laugh and I would cry and, sometimes, I would leave feeling like I had done ten rounds in the boxing ring – but every single time I left feeling a little clearer, a little more focused and a little more at ease.

Leslie helped me to realise that so much of my pain was coming from an inner story that I had carefully built over the years – that my dad didn't love me and that he saw me as a failure. She listened to this story, asked me how I had created it, why I believed it to be true, respected it. More importantly, she challenged it with love and respect but challenged it to see which parts were actually true and which parts were simply an inner, self-created story.

As we carefully investigated this inner story, I realised that there was a huge part of it that was mine and didn't actually carry any truth when looked at from a different perspective. Leslie gave me a whole new way of understanding and deconstructing my inner stories and emotions, and of realising that, in the clear light of day, most of them were simply not true and were self-created weapons of self-punishment that were totally unnecessary and that the only one holding them was me.

My work with Leslie also made me realise the importance of self-accountability and responsibility.

After we had gone through my past and my relationship with my dad to a point where the healing was done and there was little reason to keep going back into the past, I started going back into it again during a session that I will never forget. As I was speaking about my dad, Leslie leaned forward and asked if she could stop me for a moment. The look on her face let me know that no-nonsense Leslie was in the room, and rightly so. Looking me right in the eyes and holding a powerful space, she said:

Gerry, we have gone back into your past, we have worked through and I think we have healed it. We have spoken about your dad and I think we have done a great job. I also think it's time we left the past where it is and started to look at the present and the future. I think it's time you asked yourself a simple question: 'Will I always allow my past to shape my future or will I let it go and create a future that I am capable of and a future I deserve?'

It's time we started to shape your present and your future and to do that, I think we need to let go of the past with love and with gratitude for all that it was, all that it gave you and for bringing you to this point. Your past brought you here but what brings you to your future is completely up to you.

It was immediately terrifying but also liberating. I had a therapist who was challenging me in the most beautiful way to become the author of my own life, my own story and my own future. It was the first time in my life I actually realised that my past could be left behind and my future could be anything I wanted it to be; the time of blaming others was over, the time of hanging on to my past was over. Leaving her room that day I began to realise that my future could be anything I wanted it to be.

In Chapter 2, where we explored the importance of letting go of the fear that you are not enough, we learned why we need to let go of emotional trauma, that when we begin to do this, we can free ourselves from the cycle of negative talk and self-hurt.

It is only when we are free and are willing to release ourselves from the grasp of the past, from our old stories and histories, that we are free to reach out and grab a new future. Only then can we begin to create a future that is no longer defined by or created out of the thinking, memories and beliefs of the past. We can't arrive at a new destination using the same old roads of the past.

Every single one of us has a past and, for most people, there are things that they regret and things they would like to change – but we can't because the past no longer exists. The only question you have to answer is: Are you willing to release that story, willing to let your attention be released from that event so that you can reach out and grasp a new reality, a new version of yourself?

'We can't arrive at a new destination using the same old roads of the past.'

You need to be aware that, each time

you remember something in your past, you replay it in your mind and in your brain. This means you reignite the same neuro-circuitry, the same synaptic connections that were involved when the event actually happened and you trigger the same emotions. You infect the physiology of the present with the emotion, the bio-chemicals and the neuro-circuitry of the past.

Therefore, we cannot think or act in new ways. We cannot energetically bring new things into our lives if our minds and our energy fields are consumed by the things of the past. We cannot bring a new romantic person into our life if we are energetically still connected to our former partner.

Releasing yourself from the past involves a physical, physiological, biochemical shift process that creates a new freedom, and that freedom enables us to think in new ways, to create new internal software that will have the ability to create the new reality.

If we have a past that we view or experience as negative, as long as we allow our thoughts and our emotions to be connected and consumed by it, our energy field will still be filled with those things of the past and there simply is no energetic space for us to create or manifest something new. It's time to break up with your past and embrace a whole new, more exciting you and a whole new, more exciting life.

In Part 2 of this book, we will begin to create new habits and routines that will enable you to begin to discover, reignite and reawaken your best and most authentic self.

4

Letting go of ego and labels

Most of us have a misplaced understanding of what 'ego' is and how it shows up in our lives.

Most people think that 'ego' is something to do with a person who believes they are above or better than everyone else. 'Ego' is associated with the brash and self-absorbed. In fact, this is not ego at all, this is simply self-centredness and obnoxiousness.

The following are my beliefs about the nature, the role and the dangers of the human ego.

Ego can be in full flight in the most reserved, quietest person you know. Ego is the part of us that is linked to our feelings of safety and security. Our ego is the part of us that clings to things like our past, our traumas, our memories and our beliefs, and combines all these things to give us a label for us to identify with. I am the quiet one, the one with no confidence, the one who never gets a break, the unlucky one – these are all labels we give ourselves, labels created by our ego to give us a distinct identity that is different to everyone else.

Ego is simply a human-constructed reality that is terrified that without all these labels to cling to, we will have no identity at all. It will cling to the familiar labels and convince you not to change because it is even afraid of changing identity. It needs something to separate us from everything and everyone else.

Ego is fear based and doesn't like to trust in anything other than the predictable and the familiar. It wants to keep you and your identity in the familiar past and the predictable future. In some ways, the ego is like a teacher who tells a student that they are a B student based on past results and the student takes this as some type of objective truth and spends the rest of their life in the B class. The words of the teacher became the self-fulfilling prophecy of the student.

Our ego likes to order and structure us and, by doing that, it can better predict what we will do and the choices we will make. We live within the limits of the ego.

We need to become aware of the stories and labels our ego is feeding us, and then challenge and rise above them. We are not our past. We are not the decisions we made yesterday. We are free beings, free to make new and better decisions any time we want.

The ego will very quickly dismiss anything or anyone that challenges it or risks it being exposed. If we encounter someone or something that has a different life vision, a different belief system or a different life choice, the ego will try to convince us that they are

> 'We need to become aware of the stories and labels our ego is feeding us, and then challenge and rise above them. We are not our past.'

wrong. Anything other than the thoughts, beliefs and habits that match the ones of our ego will very quickly get dismissed and we will find ourselves judging others as wrong – as hippies, as ruthless business people, as religious nuts, as too young, too old. We will simply label and dismiss everything and everyone that challenges our ego. Without ever truly exploring these different beliefs, we dismiss them instantly.

The ego will also do the same when we start to express ourselves differently. The moment we think, *Maybe I could get the job. Maybe I could write a book. Maybe I could find true love,* the ego will quickly come in and dismiss the thought because the ego only knows you as the person you are now and the person you have always been – and that person doesn't have their dream job, has never written a book and has never found love.

This 'familiar past' is where the ego thrives, and it will do everything in its power to lock and trap you into old stories and old beliefs.

To change anything about ourselves, to begin to see and speak about ourselves in a new way, to create new habits and routines, we first have to challenge and overcome our terrified ego that wants to trap us in the familiar, being the same old person having the same old experiences.

The ego can also be the manifestation of a frustrated, frightened spirit. It thrives on attack and competition, and an over-ignited ego finds compromise and surrendering very difficult, even if this is surrendering to love, to the needs of a loved one, to putting the needs of another ahead of our own, and especially to accepting and believing that we are at our best and most alive when we are no longer focused on the service of self but in the connection to, and service of, something bigger than ourselves.

Ego is also an artificial construction, a sense of separateness; it's almost like a spoiled or insecure child that needs constant energy and attention to be maintained because anything else makes our fragile ego feel alone and unworthy. The ego constantly needs something to possess, and even if we don't become aware of the ego, it will eventually come to possess us.

When we surrender our ego, there is nothing to defend, nothing to maintain, no familiar past to cling to and no predictable future to strive towards, there is nothing to compare ourselves to, nothing to live in the shadow of.

By dissolving the ego, we let the mask down and replace it with our true selves, as we are and without judgement. When we dissolve the ego, we can then let go of the need to control ourselves, those around us and/or our environment, and the need to understand and the need to predict. By dissolving the ego, we can begin to live comfortably in the space between the no longer and the not yet. Without ego we become free to simply be.

Ways to dissolve and let go of ego:

- practise forgiveness and letting go
- practise honesty and being open to criticism and feedback
- surrender your need for control
- practise non-judgement of others and yourself
- commit to not making comparisons
- practise gratitude.

While there may be limitations in the physical body and the physical world, we also possess an infinite spiritual dimension that often enables us to rise above our physical limitations and experience an inner spiritual sense of freedom, love and peace. This is something that the fragile ego can't accept or believe in. Our fragile, finite ego is terrified of our true nature and tries to fight it off, dismiss it and suppress it.

To expose our fragile ego to our true reality, to the true and infinite aspect of ourselves, is to expose it to something that it simply doesn't understand. Like a caterpillar that transforms into an unrecognisable butterfly, when we dissolve the ego with a spiritual awakening, we have a deep realisation that we are all not, in fact, merely physical beings but also spiritual beings having a physical experience.

When we dissolve the created human ego, we can begin to experience a connection to something greater and bigger than our physical world. Eliminating the perception of separateness is to eliminate the need to be seen, the need to be right, and replace it with a desire to be immersed in something greater and bigger than ourselves. To eliminate this sense of separateness, we must simply realise what quantum physics is telling us – that every single thing in the universe is connected at all times. You are forever connected to this incredible universe and you can never be outside it. The more we start to build an inner connection to the self, the more we start to waken to the scientific facts of the connectedness of the universe, and the more our hearts and minds open up to the reality of connection.

Just like a wave is not afraid to return to the sea because it knows that, at all times, it is the sea, when we dissolve the ego we are able to return to our true being knowing that it is in this greater connected universal vision that we most belong.

I believe that the gateway into feeling a more powerful connection to something greater starts with dissolving the ego and reminding ourselves that we are simply a part of a masterpiece so big that we cannot understand it fully, or control it, and trusting that something or someone is guiding this bigger picture. When we release ourselves from the fear of the ego and replace it with a trust and faith in the universe, we are on the path to emotional freedom.

5

Letting go of your constructed self

I was discovering that if I was to have a chance of living a life of more and consistent presence and ease, then I could no longer cling to the constant need for external approval.

I could no longer live by constantly racing towards some new future goal and thinking that meeting that goal was going to finally make me happy. I had set thousands of goals and had met all of them; none had made me happy. I had to finally look a little deeper and address the inner need I had to be continually distracted. I had to look to the one person who really knew the answer, the one person who really knew what was going on in my head and in my heart. The one person who really knew the source of my inner pain. I had to look inwards and stop running, I had to come home to myself. Wherever we are in the world, wherever we are working from, our first and most important home is our inner self and it was time for me to come home.

I had to get to know myself in a whole new way; not just the parts of me that I liked and showed to the world, I had to really open up to all the parts of me and finally bare my soul to myself.

I was the person who was going to have to listen to my own inner thoughts, make my life decisions. I was going to spend the rest of my life with myself. Yet I had no idea who that person was.

It was no wonder I had always felt alone and lonely. If you don't know who you are, if you don't have a strong and committed relationship with your inner self, you will spend your life looking for other people to tell you who you are, and chasing goals and careers that other people said were important. You will allow yourself to be treated in any way that other people want to treat you and, when there is no external person to direct you or affirm you, you will feel lonely and alone.

The purpose of tribe and letting go of the tribe that no longer serves you

To live is to create an identity. Early in your life, you discover a role, a way of behaving, a way of speaking, a way of thinking and acting that makes you feel accepted by the people around you. Something that makes you feel that you fit in.

You take on being a person who may not be your true self, but a self that means you're accepted by the people around you – and there is a good reason for this.

In the early days of our history, when humans occupied a very dangerous world full of dangerous animals, it was important that we lived in packs or tribes. Being part of a tribe meant we were surrounded by other people, we had a strength in numbers. This tribe enabled us to hunt and to defend our habitats. Being left out of, or being left behind by, a tribe meant that we were alone and exposed. Without the tribe, we were less likely to survive.

Inbuilt in our survival programming is a protective urge to feel part of a tribe. At our deepest essence, we are social beings, born for community. As we grow and begin to develop a deeper understanding of who we really are, as we grow in confidence and realise there are very few dangerous animals to attack us, we should be able to decide which tribe, which community, we belong to, and which community best connects with our inner beliefs and ambitions. As we grow and change through life, we may very well be in different communities at different times – and this is a healthy thing.

We falsely value social affirmation as more important than self-expression

If we don't really know who we are, how do we know which community is the best for us to belong to? Without knowing who we truly are, we simply try to fit into the tribes or communities most immediate to us, or the ones other people – our friends or family – say we should be part of.

Even if we have a feeling that these communities don't actually fit our inner beliefs and desires, the sad thing is that we begin to value social affirmation as more important than self-expression and we decide to bend and shape our identity and our self-expression not in ways that express our true self, but simply in ways that get us accepted by others. We surrender the quest of becoming our true self and we commit to a lifelong quest of becoming what others want us to be and chasing things we think they want us to have.

We surrender our true self and the constructed self is born. We put on the mask for ever more, to hide behind the constructed self.

> 'The sad thing is that we begin to value social affirmation as more important than self-expression and we decide to bend and shape our identity and our self-expression not in ways that express our true self, but simply in ways that get us accepted by others.'

Hiding behind the mask of the constructed self

If we fear that our inner, truest self isn't good enough, if we have had an experience where someone – a parent, a teacher, a friend – has made us feel not good enough, if we begin to see the things that make us different and unique as wrong, we will begin to think that our true self is something to be hidden, something to be buried for fear of further rejection.

We humans are masters of adaptation. We quickly begin to adapt our thinking, feeling and behaviour until such time as we start to receive rewards and affirmation from our external tribe. When we sense that we are getting external affirmation, this motivates us to suppress our true self even more. Each time we act in accordance with what the tribe rewards, this way of thinking, acting and feeling is reinforced.

You may very well repeat this process a number of times, leaving your true self truly buried and suppressed, and the new constructed version of yourself, the one you identify with and respond to, is the one you display to the world. This constructed self is now the mask you hide behind.

Living life trying to suppress the insuppressible

Some people will spend their lives constantly trying to suppress their true self and keep it buried. They will do this with an overload of work, distraction, alcohol and an unhealthy need for social affirmation, but they will always know and feel that something is missing, something isn't right.

They will live their entire lives trying to suppress the insuppressible and rejecting their true self.

This inner rejection of self, this constant need to prove ourselves, this constant need to be seen and be respected, this constant and obsessive need to have artificial power, has led to so many of the greatest human catastrophes – including war, where innocent lives are lost over things that we don't understand, and starvation in a world where there is more than enough food and resources for everyone and yet one half stockpiles and wastes while the other half starves.

What if we could all accept who we are fully without the need for others to accept who we are? What if we didn't need to be right all the time? What if we realised we are all intimately connected and that what we do to each other, we do to ourselves?

A country cannot know full peace until it becomes free. A people cannot know full peace if they are governed by an oppressor dictating how they should think, act and feel, suppressing or denying their true identity and traditions.

As individuals, we are the same. The constructed self is the oppressor, dictating to our true self how we should think, act, feel and live, and, as long as we are willing to allow our true self to be oppressed by our constructed self, we too will never know inner peace.

Recognising the roles we are addicted to playing

When we play a role that gets us external affirmation, we feel accepted and valued by others, and we will continue to play that role even if it only gets us accepted by others and not by ourselves. The more we are affirmed for playing this role as a child, the more we continue to play this role into our adult life.

These roles we play can vary. We can be the peacemaker, the problem-solver, the person who gets things done, the person who takes on everybody else's problems or the person who always makes other people happy, saying yes to everyone else's happiness even if that means saying no to our own. We become so comfortable playing these roles that we forget that this may not be our true self. We continue to play these roles all our life and continue to be who we need to be for others – never who we need to be for ourselves.

Important questions to ask yourself are: What is the role you tend to play in most relationships? Do you find yourself playing the same role again and again? Are you tired playing this role? Is there a better role you would prefer to play?

Then ask yourself: Who is actually keeping you in this role? Who can and will give you permission to stop playing it?

There are questions I use when helping clients unlock who

they truly are, not just to help them identify their constructed self but also to enable them to let this constructed self go:

- Who are you addicted to being?
- What are the roles you play over and over again?
- Are these roles really serving you?
- What are you addicted to?
- What and who is actually imprisoning you?
- What would releasing yourself from this constructed self do for you? How would it feel?
- What would worrying less about what others think of you do for you?
- What would it take for you to give yourself permission to do this?

TAKE A MOMENT

Take some time to answer these questions in your journal.

- Can you identify the roles that you play in your family and your relationship? Are you the peacemaker, the problem-solver, the listener, the go-getter, the minder?
- When did you inherit or first start playing these roles?
- Are these roles igniting your soul and your personality or suppressing them?
- What would it take for you to surrender and let go of these roles?

- Who are you addicted to being?
- Are you someone who is always in a panic or finds themselves in chaotic situations of stress and worry?
- What are the situations you tend to find yourself in regularly?
- Who are the types of people who tend to keep appearing and reappearing in your life?
- What part of you is in some way contributing to and attracting these people or situations into your life?
- What would beginning to break this cycle of addiction require you to do and who would it require you to become?
- Do you love yourself enough to begin to free yourself from these addictions?

Try the following affirmations:

- I choose to free myself from playing self-limiting roles that no longer serve me.
- I choose to end my energetic attachment to these types of people and situations.
- I ask and give permission to the universe to cut my bonds and cords of attachment from these roles, these people and these situations.
- I energetically invite and allow myself to be free from my addictions and free to take on a new way of being.

6

Letting go of restrictive mindsets

One of the most powerful books I have discovered is *Man's Search for Meaning* by Viktor Frankl. I read it during my time in hospital and it resonated so much with me. At that time in my life, I felt restricted by so many things and I believed that different external factors in my life were holding me back and causing me unhappiness. After reading Frankl's book, I began to realise that the thing that can restrict our happiness is our mind.

This was the book that showed me the power and freedom of the human mind, and how our mind cannot actually be imprisoned when we are not imprisoning it ourselves. It showed me that when our minds and hearts begin to connect around new emotions such as love and passion and let go of anger and fear, we are capable of so much more than we ever imagined.

Viktor Frankl was an Austrian psychiatrist and a survivor of Nazi concentration camps. He was first placed in the

Theresienstadt camp with his parents, wife and brother – his father died there. Over the course of three years, he was moved between four concentration camps, including Dachau and Auschwitz. While in Auschwitz, he lost his brother and his mother. He also lost his wife, who died in the Bergen-Belsen concentration camp.

In these camps, he was subjected to some of the most harrowing experiences imaginable and yet, in an incredible decision, determined that these experiences and this loss would not be the defining point of his life. He found a way to awaken a mindset that could rise above what had happened and find inner peace.

Frankl went on to create a form of therapy he called 'logo therapy'. It is built on the premise that one of the most powerful driving forces in humans is to find meaning in our lives. That meaning, he believed, is not in the outside world but within ourselves; it is subjective and it is up to each of us to define the meaning in and of our own lives.

His work also focuses on the subjective power of choice we all have. Reading Frankl's book was the first time I had really understood that we all, in every situation, have a powerful choice – regardless of our external situation, regardless of what happens to us, we all have an individual, subjective ability to choose our response and find the meaning in our own existence.

As difficult as this may sound at first, it is actually one of the doors to transforming how we think, act and feel. It is difficult because many of us have things that have happened to us that

'We can live for so long without realising that it isn't the external world that is causing and maintaining our inner emotions and state of mind, it is our interpretation, our analysis and our reaction to what is happening to us that is actually driving our inner world.'

were unfair or even tragic, things that we have every right to be angry and bitter about. It is not always easy to let go of these things and let go of our right to be angry or bitter, but Frankl showed me the incredible power of what can happen when we do.

All too often, we can see ourselves as victims of the things that have happened to us, and we believe that we are hardwired to respond in a certain way. We think that our inner world, our thoughts and emotions, are a response driven by the external world. We can live for so long without realising that it isn't the external world that is causing and maintaining our inner emotions and state of mind, it is our interpretation, our analysis and our reaction to what is happening to us that is actually driving our inner world.

In *Man's Search for Meaning*, Frankl states:

Everything can be taken from a man but one thing: the last of the human freedoms – to choose one's attitude in any given set of circumstances, to choose one's own way.

Freedom is more important than rights

Very often in my current work, I meet clients who may be experiencing or living in a difficult external environment or may have experienced something in their past that was traumatic. I might meet them years after the trauma, but they are still full of anger and hatred or feel other destructive emotions. When we talk through their situation or their past, they will often say that they have every right to be angry, bitter or feel the way they

> 'Do you realise the impact and the damage you are doing to yourself, your quality of life and your dreams by allowing yourself to be consumed by these emotions?'

do. I agree with them completely, they do have every right to be feeling those emotions and harbouring those thoughts.

But then I ask a question: 'Do you realise the impact and the damage you are doing to yourself, your quality of life and your dreams by allowing yourself to be consumed by these emotions?'

After all, if we choose to feel and harbour certain emotions, then we are the ones who are actually experiencing the damage they cause. Holding on to negative or destructive emotions towards someone else, towards a situation or towards your past is the same as holding on to a hot coal so that you can burn someone else. The very fact that you are holding the hot coal means that you are the one getting burned.

We all have an absolute right to feel these emotions, but what many of us either don't know or don't exercise is our absolute freedom to change them.

Every emotion we express towards another is an emotion that we have to create and maintain within ourselves. We are the ones who feel that emotion first and most often.

Every emotion we hold towards someone else is an emotion

> 'We must understand the emotions we are holding on to and ask if these emotions are helping us evolve or are holding us back, trapped in the past.'

we have to experience and endure as we are the ones holding it.

We must begin to understand the emotions we are holding on to and ask if these emotions are opening our minds or closing them, opening our hearts or closing them, and whether these are emotions that are helping us evolve or are holding us back, trapped in the past.

We don't always get to choose what happens to us in life. Sometimes, we get things we never expected or wished for, things we can't control, but what we absolutely do get to control is our response to those things. We can spend the rest of our life angry and bitter but, if we do, it is *our* life we are damaging. We need to ask ourselves two questions:

- What does holding on to that anger and bitterness do to us?
- Why are we choosing to maintain that anger?

We must never underestimate or eliminate the importance of personal responsibility; it is as important as personal freedom.

We must take responsibility for our reaction to what has happened to us. If we surrender our power to choose a response that is different from or better than the things that happen to us, or the situation we find ourselves in, then we simply become the same as or equal to the situation or the person that we are reacting to.

Of course, this is a difficult thing, especially when people have had things forced on them by others, or when they have been caused serious pain or hurt by others. It's not easy to tell people in this situation that they need to move on and choose a different response – but just because it's not easy doesn't mean it's not the right thing to do.

Sometimes, we have to decide if we are going to be continually trapped in the past, trapped in a cycle of thinking and feeling that is not allowing us to be at our best or achieve the happiness and peace we crave and deserve.

W.I.N. – What's Important Now

The concept of W.I.N. is very important for me. In order to win in life, we need to know What's Important Now. This goes back to the idea that we are able to choose our response.

Sometimes, a pilot in the cockpit of an aircraft is relaxed and everything is going well, when suddenly an engine stops. The pilot could spend the next ten minutes thinking this is highly unfair. Thinking that their uncle flew for this airline for fifty years and this never happened to him. They could waste time wondering why it is happening to them now. They could get lost in a narrative of inner story that is not actually relevant, they are responding emotionally to something that is not even happening outside their mind. In this situation, the pilot is responding to a narrative and not the fact. Given that an engine has stopped: What's Important Now? 'I need to shift the fuel. I need to alter the course. I need to plot a new course and find a new runway.'

If you're attentive to the stuff that you can control, then your likelihood of success is far greater.

Yet, so many of us spend so much time thinking and talking about stuff that we can't control.

I help clients to always identify and focus on what is in their control. What can they influence?

Do not allow your energy to be sapped or sucked in by things you have no control over. People who are accountable, people who are high performers, tend to put their time and energy into things they can control.

Even if whatever has happened isn't what you expected and is not what you want – if it happened, it happened. So, we have to accept that it happened and quickly make a decision about how to respond to it.

We all possess this incredible ability to choose our response and yet so many people rarely or never exercise it. So many people feel victim to their job, their boss, their past, etc. You may ask why. There are many reasons of course but one of the biggest is that many people are sleepwalking through life. Sleepwalking in a subconscious slumber, from one day to the next, following old habits, beliefs and ways of thinking.

In order to begin to exercise our powerful ability to choose, we must first wake up – we must fall awake in consciousness and out of subconscious sleepwalking.

For many, these are terms they have heard millions of times, but what really is the subconscious mind? What is consciousness? The truth is we have many states of consciousness and when we begin to understand them and waken them, something amazing happens. It's time to waken your consciousness and, when you do, things will never be the same again.

I will explore and explain in Chapter 12 the nature of the various levels of our consciousness and how you can fully waken and utilise each level in a powerful way.

7

Letting go of our old thinking habits and creating new brain pathways

Our brain is immutable and we have the ability to change both our brain structure and our thinking patterns. Most skills are built by repetition, and thinking is no different. The more we think in a certain way, the more we build the habit of that thinking pattern. Neuroscience has proven that our brain is changeable, and this means that we are not born with a brain that is hardwired or unchangeable but we are born with a brain that is open to, and capable of, vast change.

'Neuroplasticity' is the term used to describe this change in neural pathways and synapses in your brain that occurs because of certain factors, such as behaviour, environment or neural processes. During such changes, your brain engages in synaptic pruning, which is a deleting of the neural connections that are no longer necessary or useful and the strengthening of the ones you use most.

Put simply, neuroplasticity is the ability of the brain to

constantly reshape itself in response to what you say, what you listen to and what you think about.

Your brain has the incredible ability to change and create new thinking pathways, but only if you consciously make it. Otherwise, your lazy brain is happy to stick with the familiar and the easy.

'Neuroplasticity is the ability of the brain to constantly reshape itself in response to what you say, what you listen to and what you think about.'

Each time you have the same thought, you fire that specific brain pathway and send an electrical signal through it, and each time you fire that pathway the entire pathway is wrapped in a substance called myelin. This makes that specific pathway bigger and thicker. Think of myelin as insulation that gets wrapped around a pipe. Each layer makes it bigger and bigger.

Your brain is incredible, but it is lazy. Your brain will simply keep going to the pathways that are easiest to find. Of course, the ones that are easiest to find are the ones wrapped in the most myelin. It's a self-perpetuating pattern.

I realised that I needed to change my thinking habits and patterns. I knew that we are all capable of changing our thoughts and the shape and makeup of our brains. We can build new pathways in our brains that enable us to think and respond in all-new ways.

I needed to change my inner story. I needed to change my inner script and create new thinking habits – and I did.

I created a new inner reality filled with new images, new words and new emotions through the power of a mental training tool called 'visualisation'.

Visualisation is a powerful practice to build greater inner resilience, motivation and performance, and helps manifest your goals, dreams and desires. It is the process of creating a mental image or clear intention of what you want to happen or feel in reality. We can use this technique to prepare and rehearse a desired outcome or simply to rest in a relaxed feeling of calm and well-being.

When we perform a visualisation exercise, we can actually stimulate the same brain regions as we would if we were physically performing the task. Visualisation changes how your brain networks are organised, creating more synaptic connections among different regions.

Visualisation is about building the neuro-circuitry required to execute certain skills or deal with certain situations in advance to ensure that when we encounter them for real, we have the internal skills and networks that will enable us to have the thinking and actions we need to achieve the outcomes we desire. By building these new brain circuits, we are literally building a whole new mental response and new mental programmes.

Visualisation is firstly an internal exercise where you use the power of your own mind to create these inner images and visions, but visualisation can also be helped by some external tools, such as a vision board.

Becoming aware of our thinking habits and internal stories and programmes

We have to become conscious of our thinking patterns and habits and then, not only have to *stop* thinking in that way, but also *start* thinking and acting in new ways.

CREATE YOUR OWN VISION BOARD

A vision board is a collage of images, dreams and ideas that you carefully create and put together that represents the best, most ignited version of you, and is a vision of what you want and aspire your life to look and feel like.

A vision board is one of the most valuable visualisation tools available to you. The inspirational collages serve as your image of the future. It should represent your dreams, your goals and your ideal life. Creating your own vision board is an incredible way of keeping your goals, dreams and ideas at the forefront of your mind, keeping you inspired and motivated. These images help flood your subconscious mind with new images, and the subconscious mind doesn't know the difference between real and imaginary. The more feel-good, positive images you feed your subconscious mind, on a moment-by-moment basis, the more these images become a reality.

We will explore the exact nature of the subconscious mind in Chapter 12.

So, get creative! Cut out words, visions and images from magazines and newspapers, print out empowering pictures or phrases that sing to your heart. When you have them, place them on your board.

The first thing to help us in this process is identifying how we create enough silence to hear our own thoughts so that we can then identify the habits and patterns we need to change.

It may be surprising to many that we can actually hear our own thoughts – and it is easier than we may think, if we are willing to put time and practice into it.

I created this time and practice through meditation.

Meditation

The word 'meditation' can make us think of monks in robes, sitting in a temple chanting for hours, but it can also create inner frustration as it seems to be used a million times a day by all types of people making all types of claims about the power of the practice.

So, let's take a simple and honest look at meditation, what it is and what it does.

It's important in our modern world that we have a modern understanding and application for meditation. We do not need to be monks to have meditation as part of our everyday experience and, at the same time, we do not need to be experts at it.

There are many types of meditation and all have equal power depending on:

- The purpose – Do you know what you want from your meditation?
- The commitment – Are you willing to commit to it?

- The openness – Are you open to it and open to the power of it?
- The type – Have you tried different types?

In many ways, *you* are as important as the meditation practice and more important than the person leading the meditation practice.

If you don't work at meditation, the meditation does not work.

Most people fall down with meditation because they simply don't commit to it or they are not open to it or do not know what they want from it.

In its simplest form, meditation is the art of training your mind to generate an image and hold that image without being distracted by external or internal sources. Meditation is about being attentive to one thing at one time and training your concentration muscle.

Meditation can also be where you are conscious of and observing your senses and the stimuli around you without getting emotionally attached or distracted by them. Meditation can be where we are focused on one thing or aware of many things but the goal of meditation is the emotional experience we generate within – this is an experience of calm, letting go of resistance, letting go of anger or frustration, and replacing it with a feeling of ease and peace.

The more time you can spend on moments or sustained periods experiencing emotional ease, calm and security, the more

'If you don't work at meditation, the meditation does not work.'

you enable your brain and your central nervous system to come out of the distracted, over-agitated, fight-or-flight state.

This enables you to activate the neocortex of your brain, which allows greater imagination and decision-making and a far greater perspective. Getting out of the fight-or-flight state stops you being imprisoned by your limbic, stress-based brain that operates only from your unconscious beliefs and programmes.

When your brain is no longer in a fight-or-flight state, your central nervous system can rebalance and repair, and this has incredible physical and mental benefits. This feeling of safety and inner ease reduces the production and presence of certain key hormones in your system, such as cortisol and adrenaline. We know from research that high levels of cortisol and adrenaline negatively impacts our immune systems, which leaves us susceptible to viruses and diseases.

Meditation is a simple way of reducing stress and stress hormones. It is a simple way of elevating an inner sense of safety that results in boosting our immune systems.

There are many types of meditation, from seated to standing to walking. There is guided meditation, when we are guided by a voice, and there are non-guided meditations when we are guided only by our own breath or by a feeling of presence that is outside ourselves.

Meditation for me was the thing that removed me from all external noise, distraction and expectations and enabled me to discover and build my true inner voice and emotions – my own true inner self. By taking time to go inwards, I was no longer relying on external things to affirm or guide me. I now had an important and sacred internal reservoir from which I could draw calmness, confidence and belief, regardless of my external world.

The exciting realisation in this is another simple question: If we are listening to our own thoughts, and thoughts are happening in the brain, then which part of us is listening to our thoughts?

Which part of you is outside your brain listening to the thoughts of your brain? The answer is the part of you that is the observer and not the experience, the part of you that is conscious that your brain is thinking.

When we learn to become present, when we learn to stop judging, resisting and fighting what is happening without getting overly emotionally connected or attached to it, when we are no longer simply the experience, the conditioned reflex, but become the observer in our own life, we open up a new and incredible ability – the ability to choose a new or different path.

We begin to see ourselves and the world through a different lens. When you become the observer in your own life, you can see it in a more clear and honest way. Becoming the observer gives you a new and greater perspective in which you make new and better decisions.

Becoming the observer means that you are no longer the person who life is happening *to* and who is spending their life in a reactive state, but the person who life is happening *for*, the person who is proactively making their life go in the direction they are consciously creating. In this state, you become the creator of your future and not a replay of your past.

Becoming the observer in your own life is about making an important discovery: you are not defined by the things that happen to you, but by the decisions you make and by the response you choose.

Becoming the observer in our own lives gives us a powerful ability to choose our response to any situation. Not being overly emotionally committed or connected to what is happening, or what has happened, in our lives gives us the emotional capacity to let go all that no longer serves us.

Every situation that happens in our lives is simply a picture and, as the observer, we have the mental freedom to decide which part of that picture, which part of any situation, we choose to focus on. We get to decide where we place our emotions and our thoughts and we get to decide where we place our focus and energy.

We get to decide which thoughts we attach to and which thoughts we allow to dissolve and disappear.

Breaking the cycle: addiction to our stress hormones and chemicals

Thoughts are not just thoughts, they have a chemical and electrical dimension that is really important to be aware of in order to understand how we can actually become addicted to certain thinking habits and patterns. We know that certain thoughts and emotions cause the body and the brain to produce different chemicals in the form of neurotransmitters that then cause changes in the body, just like any drug.

Stressful or fearful emotions signal the brain and body to produce many important neurotransmitters and hormones such as cortisol and adrenaline. These neurotransmitters and hormones are powerful and addictive chemicals – and, the more we have in our body, the more we will crave them. What is even more important is that the more often we experience cortisol and adrenaline in our system, the more we become desensitised to them.

This means that each time they are released, we will start to need more of them to enable us to feel the same reaction. Subconsciously, we start to seek out more and more stressful environments and stressful situations that will release the stress chemicals we crave.

As bizarre as it sounds, we will seek out situations and information that make us feel anxious. We wake up and, instantly, we will begin to crave them so we will immediately be drawn to our phones where we will search through work emails, social media, various news outlets until we find things that we can be stressed about or annoyed about. We are doing this because our bodies are craving some type of stressful situation or stressful news so it can release the stress hormones that we have become addicted to.

There are also powerful substances that the brain and body can produce that have a very positive effect on our minds and bodies. Oxytocin is a very powerful hormone produced by the pituitary gland. It is known as the snuggle hormone because it is released when people cuddle or hug, or even when they feel an emotion of being loved or connected.

'Often our bodies are the victims of our thoughts and emotions – and when we change the nature of our thoughts and emotions, we change our physiology and our chemistry.'

Oxytocin has the ability to regulate our emotional responses and increase our pro-social behaviours and emotions, such as trust, empathy, processing of bonding cues, and positive communication.

When I look back at my younger self, no one ever explained to me that there was a chemical impact and consequence of my thoughts and thinking habits – and no one told me that if I could break the thinking habits and addictions, I would go from having a system high on cortisol and stress hormones to a system that was flooded in hormones that made me feel more at peace and more at ease in pro-social activities. To understand the impact our thoughts and emotions can have on the hormones that are flooding our system and making changes in our bodies and our central nervous systems is the first step towards change. Understanding that we have the power and ability to change much of the chemical reality of our bodies simply by changing our thoughts and our emotions is an even more empowering realisation.

Very often, we are not victims of what is happening in our bodies. Often our bodies are the victims of our thoughts and emotions – and when we change the nature of our thoughts and emotions, we change our physiology and our chemistry.

MEDITATION

Set aside ten or fifteen minutes to do this meditation.

To start: Come into a nice comfortable position. You can be seated or lying down, whatever feels more comfortable and soothing for your body in the moment. When you are ready, close your eyes and turn your gaze inwards. If you don't feel comfortable closing your eyes you can simply lower your gaze or bring your awareness to the tip of your nose.

Relax your shoulders down and away from your ears and begin to soften all the muscles of your face. Release any tension or tightness from the jaw area. Soften through the front and back of the neck. Let your temples be gentle and just begin to breathe.

Without trying to change or shift your breath in any way, simply breathe – in and out of your nose, gently, slowly and softly. Feel the cool air entering through your nose, oxygenating your cells and purifying your mind. When you exhale, feel the subtle, warm air leave your body – taking with it any fears, doubts or worries. Continue to breathe in this way for a few more moments.

Then bring your awareness to your heart and lungs in the centre of your chest. We tend to hold a lot of past sadness, loss or grief in the lungs. As you breathe in and out, imagine the lungs opening and expanding with new life force and, as you exhale, imagine any old imprints of past memories or experiences that you want to let go of leaving energetically with the exhalation.

As you do this, let the following questions wash over you and observe what insights come your way.

- What is the one thing in the past that you think you are still energetically attached to?
- What or who do you need to forgive to let this go?
- What would letting this go do for your health, happiness and life?
- What is the cost of not letting this go?
- What is the first step that you need to take to begin to let this go. Is it writing a letter to someone letting them know that they are forgiven? Maybe it's writing a letter to yourself forgiving yourself or maybe it's a letter to the universe affirming that you are letting this go.
- What other external supports might you need? For example, would counselling help?

When you are ready, finish this meditation by taking five deep, slow belly breaths.

Place your hands on your heart – the centre for compassion, forgiveness, love and light. Place the intention of letting go into your heart and then breathe this out into the world.

Take as long as you need here in this space.

When you feel ready, open your eyes and take a nice, gentle stretch.

Well done.

8

Letting go of our associations with struggle

Believe it or not, we can become addicted to force and struggle. We can become addicted to the sensations of 'hard' and 'difficult'. A simple example is when we go to the gym. We believe that a good gym session is where we push ourselves to the limit and where we leave feeling tired and exhausted, even sore. We have a belief that the harder the session feels, the better the session was. We don't want a gym session to feel easy and, if it does, we feel guilty that we didn't do enough, which is simply us using our inner need to punish ourselves or tell ourselves that we are not good enough.

The questions we don't ask are: What has the session actually done for us? Has it lowered or raised our cortisol levels? What did we learn or change about ourselves in that session? Did we actually just practise and reinforce the same old habits? Did we just reinforce the same old thinking and self-talk habits? Is my life or my inner world healthier after the session?

Very often, we are happy to go to the gym without any real understanding or passion about what we are actually doing, about what we are actually hoping to change. Far too often, the gym is simply somewhere we go to work on the outer body while never connecting it with or requiring it to do anything for our inner world. We go to the gym, we push ourselves hard, we leave tired and sore and, therefore, it must have been a good session – wrong. There is actually no connection between hard and happy or sore and productive. We have created an unhealthy association between them, but they are not necessarily connected.

In life, we become addicted to the same idea. We become conditioned to the belief that life should be hard. We begin to believe being successful is about hard work and grafting it out. We believe that struggle is part and parcel of life and of success, and we couldn't possibly be successful without pain and struggle.

However, we forget that, if we observe a world-class athlete or musician or artist in full flight, in full expression of their passion and their talent, we notice that they make it look easy. The people who are truly world class at what they do, people who are doing what they love, people who are following their hearts, can achieve the most extraordinary things while making it look easy. Imagine if you saw a world-class footballer walking around the pitch with their head hanging, their body uptight, telling everyone that football was hard, that the game was hard and they were just waiting for the end of the game or that they couldn't wait for the end of the season. Do you think they would play well? Do you think their team-mates would pass them the ball? Do you think they would go on to great things?

And yet that is how we talk to ourselves. It's laughable to think of a world-class athlete thinking, speaking and behaving in the same way we do.

Of course, there is pain and struggle along the path to becoming world class but, on the whole, they love what they do and wouldn't choose to do anything else. Most of us, on the other hand, seem to have to endure pain and struggle for far longer periods, to the point where we see it as simply part of life. Not only do we not question it but we actually begin to use it as a way of giving us feedback, that we are working hard, that we are productive, that we are alive. If you seem to have struggle and pain as a regular element in your life, if you have forgotten that not only can life feel easy and peaceful but it should feel peaceful and easy, then maybe you need to ask yourself where this struggle and pain is coming from and what or who is actually the cause.

The more we look for pain, force and struggle to be part of our efforts to reinforce ourselves, the more pain and struggle will become part of everything we do. It will eventually become the norm in our lives and we will actually forget what anything else feels like.

You can spend your entire life struggling through the day waiting for the evening, struggling through the week waiting for Saturday, struggling through the month waiting for pay day, struggling through the year waiting for summer holidays or Christmas. Struggle and waiting becomes our state of being.

The more we live in the struggle mindset, the more we are energetically sending out the signal to ourselves, to the people around us and to the universe that we are not capable of taking on new or better. Living in the struggle state of mind and state of being actually has the opposite effect to what we are trying to achieve.

When we are energetically living in and sending out the signal and energy of struggle, we are living in a state that can only manifest more of the same energy, which will be more pain and struggle.

We need to break away from the belief that pain and struggle are necessary for success.

We need to break away from the belief that pain and struggle are part of life.

When we start to see that ease and grace offer a far more powerful and productive way to live and manifest our dreams, we can begin to allow ourselves to think, act and feel in a whole new way. A way of ease and peace.

If you are experiencing reoccurring pain and struggle in your life, you need to ask yourself some important questions. Is my pain and struggle coming from my need to feel pain and struggle? Is my pain and struggle caused by my reaction to, interpretation of or resistance to what is happening? Is my pain and struggle caused by the way I am choosing to go about the

'We need to break away from the belief that pain and struggle are necessary for success. We need to break away from the belief that pain and struggle are part of life.'

task? Is my pain and struggle caused by the fact that what I am doing is not in alignment with my soul's purpose and passion?

When we begin to prioritise ease and grace, we begin to rethink what we spend our time doing and how we do it. Pain and struggle are in no way connected to or necessary for success. We need to free ourselves from this unhealthy connection and wake up to the reality and the realisation that ease and grace are a far more efficient and productive ways to live our lives and manifest our dreams.

Pain may be inevitable, but struggle is optional

Finally, we must recognise that there is a big difference between pain and struggle. I for one know all too well that pain is often part of life. Things happen to us that cause pain, both physical and emotional. We all know that the loss of a loved one, the loss of a job or the breakdown of a relationship are painful experiences and very few of us get through an entire lifetime without some pain visiting us.

Struggle, however, is our reaction, our resistance, our anger towards and our inability to deal with the pain when it happens. Pain can be a part of your life, but struggle is more of your choice.

You can learn that you always have a choice, and that the choice you have is not whether pain appears in your life or not, but how you choose to respond to it. No matter what the pain is, no matter if it is something you never wanted or expected, at some point, you have to accept that it is and you have to let go of your anger and bitterness towards it. When you do, when you begin to find the courage and strength to accept that which you know, then you have the ability to choose your response.

Pain may be something you can't control, but your response to it is absolutely something you can control. Struggle, although common, is not normal or natural, and when you break up with your addiction to the need for struggle and release yourself into a place of ease and grace, you actually become so much more effective and successful.

9

Letting go of the fear of change
and the fear of the unknown

I regularly meet people who tell me that they don't like change or that they are afraid of the unknown. Yet, I have never read in a newspaper or heard on a news programme that somebody was killed or harmed by the unknown. The unknown has never really harmed anyone.

The role of the ego in resisting change and uncertainty

It is our ego, our fragile ego, that resists change and the unknown. Our ego craves the ability and is driven by the need to control, predict and understand. As we mentioned in Chapter 4, it will often trap us in the past – even if our past wasn't wonderful or had sadness or hurt in it – because at least our past is familiar. The emotions we attach to and experience about the past may be self-limiting and hurtful, but at least they are predictable and that is what our ego craves, so it will resist any possible situation or future where you are different to that past, to those thoughts, those stories and those emotions.

The ego needs something to possess, and it can eventually come to possess us and trap us in a life where we simply perpetuate the past and repeat the familiar.

When we dissolve the ego, we can then let go of the need to control, the need to understand and the need to predict. By dissolving the ego, we can begin to live comfortably in the space between the no longer and the not yet.

It is not the unknown, it's what we project into the unknown that we fear

Sometimes, when we are faced with the unknown, our minds start to race. Depending on our levels of self-belief and self-awareness, we can overestimate the challenge ahead and underestimate ourselves. When we do this, we become consumed by fear because we think we will fail. This fear starts to manifest itself in different visions about the unknown and we project these visions into the unknown. It is rarely the unknown that we fear, it is what we project into the unknown that we fear.

'It is not the unknown that we fear, what we fear is what we project into the unknown.'

The first step to understanding the power of transition and change, the power of the unknown, is to realise that we live in a world where everything is changing all the time. The earth you are standing on at this moment is spinning at 1,000 miles an hour.

Every single cell, every single atom in your body is changing and moving all the time. Right now, your heart is pumping non-stop, your blood is flowing around your body. Your lungs are taking in fresh oxygen, that's being flushed through your lungs and transformed into carbon dioxide which is then put back into the universe. Right now, your digestive enzymes are breaking down food, digesting the food and the contents of your gut. At this moment, there is a mass of neurotransmitters and chemicals flooding through your system. There is nothing stationary in your body. Everything is moving, everything is healing, everything is renewing at all times.

When we take this further, we begin to realise that even in the external world, in the physical world, things are moving all the time. If we take what appears to be a stationary object – let's say a lamppost – the lamppost seems to be stationary and not moving. Until we remember that the earth is spinning at 1,000 miles per hour and so is the lamppost. We live in a world of constant change. We project an illusion of static to protect our fragile ego.

Even when we look closer at the lamppost, if we watch it, take note of it, and do this again and again over a period of time, maybe a year or five years, we will notice that the lamppost itself is changing. Its colour changes, rust appears, which means that all the while, slowly but surely, the lamppost changes. The sea is constantly moving. New beaches are created. The truth is we live in a world of constant change where nothing is static.

The first thing we all need to do is embrace change. Change is a natural, progressive, unstoppable force of nature. It enables us to grow, to develop, to become different. In fact, it is not change that is unnatural but stagnation. If you stay in the same place for too long, if you stay being the same person for too long, your mind, your body, your spirit become stagnated. Change is not unnatural – change is perfectly natural.

So, what we all need to do is to begin to look not at the change or the unknown, but at what is known. What is the known within the unknown? The answer is you.

You are a powerful being. When you align your mind, your body and your spirit, when you awaken your dreams, when you trust in yourself, then you realise that what is inside you is far more powerful and far more important than what lies outside or ahead of you. You have an inner intelligence, an inner knowing, that can guide and move you to ever new and ever more exciting places. When you begin to listen to it and trust it.

When we commit to working on the power of the mind and to using the skills and resources at our disposal to help us to become more calm and more focused in the present, then the one commitment we can make is that no matter what lies ahead of us, in that moment when the unknown is unfolding, we will be calm, we will be focused. We will live with passion and with love and we will ask questions that awaken our consciousness: What's important now? What in this moment can I control? What in this moment, if I truly loved myself, would I be willing to do?

There is no danger in the unknown. There is nothing unnatural about change and transition. What is unnatural is to resist it, to fight it, to pretend that the world we want is a world of static non-movement. The very gift of this universe is built on its ability to move, evolve and change. The gift of your life is awakening to your incredible ability to rise and thrive in transition and change. To understand that what lies inside of you is far more powerful and important than what lies outside of you. Remember, in the face of the unknown, you are the known.

We have to make a decision: Do we focus on the unknown or do we focus on the known? You are the known and you are more powerful than the unknown when you start to awaken your heart, your mind and your soul. When you focus on you, when your energy becomes more powerful than the energy of fear, then it is no longer the unknown that is shaping you, it is you that is shaping the unknown.

When you learn to love and trust yourself, when you learn to be guided by your inner instinct, you know that, in every moment, no matter what unfolds, you have the ability, the compassion, the focus and the concentration to deal with anything. Go and embrace the unknown. Step forward, step into the uncertain and the unknown with trust, with faith and with love. Believe in yourself.

Control that which is within your control and let everything else go. However big or small the change you are facing is, embrace it with an open heart, a united spirit and an inner belief.

You were born and destined to change and grow. It is never change that stops us from living, it is our resistance to it. Embrace change with all your heart and all your soul, and in any darkness of unknown – be the light of the known.

TAKE A MOMENT

Take a moment to ask yourself a few questions.

- What is the change you would like to make?
- What would making that change bring into your lifestyle?
- What would it take out?
- What do you fear about the change?
- What is the change you are resisting?
- What is the cost of not making the change?
- What is the cost of making the change poorly?
- What or who is actually stopping you?
- Are you overestimating the challenge or underestimating yourself?

CREATE AN EXTERNAL CHANGE SUPPORT SYSTEM

- **Create a vision board**: Create a vision of the life and the successful change you desire. Focus on this every morning, focus on what you want, not what you fear.
- **Create a personality board**: Create images and words that describe the person you want to be and read them every day. Live one of those words every day.
- **Create a gratitude board**: Fill yourself with gratitude every day for the things you have right now.

- **Create an aligned micro-environment**: Ensure that it is focused on and facilitates positive change.
- **Find the person who has done (or who is doing) what you want to do**: Ask them how they did it.
- **Put yourself in the way of opportunity.**
- **Be defined, not by your fall, but by your rise.**
- **Be the person who sees their dreams even clearer when they open their eyes.**

CREATE AN INTERNAL CHANGE SUPPORT SYSTEM

- **Refocus your self-talk**: Would you say the things you say to yourself to someone you love?
- **Deconstruct excuses**: What are the excuses that you are using to explain your fear or resistance? How will you deconstruct these one at a time?
- **Visualisation**: Create the neurological hardware for success. Be inspired by your vision of the future, not your memory of the past.
- **See your why every day**: Write down a description of the future or take a picture that fires your thoughts and emotions, one that excites and inspires you and fills you with love. Create a new electrical charge that is more powerful than the original one, you can't think or perceive outside your emotional state.
- **Be aware of where you are putting your energy people**: Beware the dream-stealers and energy vampires.

- **Reframe failure**: Maybe failure is staying the same, getting stale and repeating the same things over and over – maybe failure is simply not giving yourself the opportunity to change.

- **Remember past successes**: We have all dealt with transition and change in our lives so reignite the positive ones and remember you have done it before and can do it again.

- **Examine and change your inner beliefs through self-talk and new routines**: If we do better, we feel better. If we do new, we feel new. Affirm your wins, no matter how small, every single day.

- **Practise becoming present**: Don't allow yourself to be distracted by things that are not important or things that trap you in fear or uncertainty. Break your addiction to the emotions and neurotransmitters that stress creates.

- **Simply begin**: Today is either one day or day one.

- **Manage your wellness**.

- **Today, be the type of person you would like to meet**.

- **Step into the dark and remember you are the light**.

10

Letting go of the dis-ease of distraction

The epidemic of distraction: distraction steals our health

A distracted mind is not capable of seeing the opportunities in the external world, it is limited to seeing and experiencing only the chaos inside.

As you rush around in a distracted state, there is little or no time to take in the world around you – life becomes a blur of activity that you aren't able to enjoy or be present in. In this chronic stress state, the conscious part of your brain is shut off and you are limited to operating from your unconscious mind.

We now know that when we operate from our unconscious mind, we are not really observing the world or situation as it is, we are simply projecting our inner beliefs and expectations onto the outside world, and are living in a

> 'A distracted mind is not capable of seeing the opportunities in the external world, it is limited to seeing and experiencing only the chaos inside.'

145

limited, self-created version of reality. We are no longer present or aware in our own lives. We are simply reliving old stories and old versions of reality again and again, and wondering why the same thing keeps happening to us.

We become non-thinking, perpetual-motion machines, preconditioned reflexes convinced that doing is more valuable than being. We pride ourselves on how much we get done, but we don't ask ourselves: Was I efficient? Did I enjoy doing it? Was there a better way of doing it? Is it actually what I want to be doing? Without these questions to trigger us out of this unconscious, non-thinking state of busy distraction, we continue into the next thing and the next thing, becoming more and more distracted as we go.

We get distracted by the urgent and ignore the important

In today's always-on, busy external world, we tend to be constantly giving our attention, energy and time to the things that are urgent but not important. Very often we are distracted by the immediate things of day-to-day life and rarely get a chance to get to the important things – like minding our physical and mental health, spending time with the people we love and telling them that we love them, or actually pursuing our dreams.

We get so distracted by the immediate that we even forget to ask ourselves the important questions: Am I really happy? Is there enough fun and laughter in my life? Do I actually love my job? What is it I really want from this short life?

Our life ends up revolving and not evolving

If we are attending to the immediate all the time and ignoring the important, it is quite possible that we are *revolving* in life, going around in circles, rather than *evolving* and expanding our minds, our hearts and our spirits.

Most of us rarely stop to look at our lives and ask if we are revolving or evolving. We forget to ask ourselves questions like: Am I healthier this year than last year? Have I more self-confidence this year than last? Have I more inner peace? Am I closer to my dreams?

I believe there comes a time in all our lives when revolving becomes boring. It becomes stale and, when it does, our minds and our souls become stale too, and we lose our inner spark and extinguish our inner magic.

I believe the new age of busy, the always-on phenomenon that is driving this state of constant distraction, is also leading us to experience more ill-health and lack of ease in our mind, body and soul.

> 'If we are attending to the immediate all the time and ignoring the important, it is quite possible that we are *revolving* in life, going around in circles, rather than *evolving*.'

We normalise tiredness, exhaustion and even ill-health

In this type of always-on world, where we live and think in this distracted haze, constant distraction becomes our new normal – to the point where we no longer even notice how distracted we are. We develop the dis-ease of distraction and we don't even realise it. We often live in communities of equally distracted people who can't see it either.

If you live in a community where everyone is infected with the disease of distraction, you begin to see it as a common and normal thing, but what is common is often what is not normal. We need to wake up to the truth that distraction, fatigue and busyness are not at all normal and, in fact, have a very real and damaging impact on our quality of life and our health.

We have normalised being busy and exhausted, and it now seems perfectly normal for people to be constantly in this state. It has become normal to be and to feel depleted and we don't even take a moment to think about why we are so tired.

We have come to believe – wrongly – that tiredness is simply a consequence of life. It's not, it's absolutely not. Exhaustion is a consequence of either not proactively minding our health and well-being, and not being able to switch off when we need to, or a consequence of being in a life that is simply revolving and has become stale and boring.

It is perfectly OK for life to be about vitality, fun, laughter, passion and inner peace. Very often, it's not life that exhausts us, it's the decisions we make about and in life.

The problem is that because you are moving at such pace – revolving at such a pace – you never get the chance to step off the treadmill, and this is what will drive your ill-health in so many ways. If you live a life where you allow yourself to be constantly activated and busy and hold emotions of fear or attack, you are burning yourself out.

Take, for example, an athlete who trains and trains, and then runs a big race, but doesn't take time out after to rest, rehydrate, recover and rehab – they won't be able to continue to perform at their best. They will simply burn out. It's the same with life. We are like the athlete, continuously going and going but never allowing ourselves the chance to get off the track, to rest and recover.

It is time to ask ourselves if we are focusing on the urgent or the important.

Investing in our health

If we don't take time to invest in our health, we will be forced to take the time to invest in our sickness.

This level of distraction has two main issues. First, it takes us out of the present moment and stops us from enjoying each moment as it unfolds. It keeps us locked into a swing where our mind is constantly moving between the past and the future and misses the present, thereby preventing us from slowing down long enough to identify or become our true selves.

Our lives can pass us by and we're not even aware of it.

Valuable, priceless moments are happening right in front of us, moments that may never happen again, and we might be missing them completely.

The second issue is the very real and profound impact this level of distraction has on our physical health and well-being.

We must invest our time wisely

We must also be aware that distraction is constantly taking us out of the moment, so that what should be our life becomes a blurred reality. The opportunity to be happy, to be at ease and to experience joy exists only in the present moment. The more distracted we are, the less ease, peace and joy we experience. This becomes especially important when we begin to realise how short life is and how special each and every moment is.

Create a healthy relationship with time and remember it's 900

In our modern world, we are bombarded with so many numbers – the number of steps we need to walk in a day, the number of calories we need to eat and then burn, the number of hours we need to sleep, the number of pieces of fruit we are meant to eat per day: the numbers never seem to stop. Yet, in my experience, there is only one number that inspires me and motivates me every day of my life. In fact, I think it's the most important number for all of us and when we hear it our eyes, ears, minds and hearts immediately pay attention to it. The magic number is 900.

The average human lifespan is only 900 months. If that shocks you, wait a second.

Out of that 900 we sleep 300. We have approximately 600 waking months on this planet and, depending on your age right now, you can quickly work out roughly how many months you have left.

As shocking and frightening as this may be, it is also liberating. What is even more shocking is how few people take a moment to realise how special time is, and how special each day and each month is.

I experienced this incredible realisation during my time

in hospital. It shocked me, and motivated me to begin to truly appreciate how precious my time was. I also realised that none of us ever knows exactly how much or how little time we will get. Most of us don't treat time with the respect and sacredness it deserves. We allow our time to be filled with things that are not really important in the long term or in the bigger picture.

When I ask people what the most important things in their lives are, most will answer: my parents, my children, my siblings, my loved ones and my health.

Then I ask them what three things take up most of their time, and the answer is often very different. In a world where we are often rushing to the future – to the weekend, to Christmas, to summer – we need to be careful that we are not rushing and wishing our life away.

Beware of the time and energy thieves

We have 168 hours every single week. That never changes and yet ask most people to account for their 168 hours and they can't – in spite of feeling like they have no spare time.

For most of us, twenty to thirty hours each week go missing. We lose, on average, one day every week because we are distracted or we are spending more time on things that I call 'time thieves'. We are unconsciously scrolling our time away, watching meaningless television shows or doing things that are not actually adding value or happiness to our lives, but which use up our valuable time.

I now see how precious each moment, each conversation, each hug and each breath are. I promised myself one major thing when I was in hospital: when I left, I was finally going to start living in a whole new way. No more wasting time on unimportant things, no more waiting for someone to give me permission to start living my life, no more time for regrets. I promised myself that I would become much more present in my own life, more present in each day and in each moment. I would no longer take time or experiences for granted. I identified the things that I will miss most when I am gone, and I promised to cherish them while I am still here.

With each hug, I have learned to take an extra second to really feel it in case it is my last with that person. I vowed to extract as much joy and ease as I possibly could from each moment. I was going to start being more selective about the things I would allow to take up my time and energy, about the things I would invest my precious time and energy into.

For me, this was another big wake-up call. I had spent so much of my time rushing and focusing on the wrong things, chasing the wrong things and giving my time to the wrong things. Because I was chasing external approval, I was chasing the things other people wanted and not the things I really wanted. Because I was always chasing, always distracted, I had never even taken the time to stop and actually ask myself what I really wanted and what was important to me.

I had been so distracted with the world outside of me, I'd never taken the time to listen to my inner world. I was so busy trying to impress everyone else, I was simply chasing whatever everyone else was chasing. I began to ask if it was possible to slow down time and if it was possible to live in a way that would enable me to experience more of the right things in the time I have.

Of course, the answer is yes. It is absolutely possible.

We can't slow the time of the clock down – sixty seconds is always sixty seconds – but we can slow down and expand our experience within those sixty seconds.

If you have ever had to wait a week for a really important piece of information, then you will know that that week can feel like a month. We also know that if we ever had to wait an hour to find out if we had a serious illness, that hour would feel like a lifetime. It is not that time speeds up, it is our minds. It is not the clock that starts rushing, it is our attention.

I started to learn how to slow down time. I started to understand the power of the breath and how many of us are breathing in a threat state. In this state, we breathe far too quickly and far too shallowly. We should be taking eight to ten breaths a minute, but many of us are taking twenty-plus.

Our incredible lungs have a capacity of approximately six litres. Yet many of us are only breathing from the top of our lungs and using only a fraction of our capacity. This fast, shallow, threat-state breathing triggers us into a mental, chemical and physiological threat state and we lose our conscious ability to be present, to truly observe, and to concentrate.

The more I researched and practised optimal breathing – some call it belly breathing or diaphragmatic breathing – the more I realised that the very simple act of becoming aware of my breath and slowing it down allowed my whole being to slow down, and as I slowed down and became more present, I was able to become far more aware of each moment and I had the ability to expand time.

I never imagined the power that something so simple could have. I was finally starting to become present and consciously awake to the potential of my own life, a life that was truly mine. By using my breath to slow down my mind and pay closer attention to the power of the breath, I realised that our breath, and the way in which we breathe, is actually a central component of how we feel in both our minds and our bodies.

The incredible power of our breath has so many important features that we must awaken to and begin to harness. Our bodies are designed to release toxins through our breath. We exhale nitrogen, oxygen, argon and carbon dioxide. A build-up of toxins in our body can manifest in increased illness, acute and chronic pain, and many other physical imbalances.

We all have this amazing tool and ability at our disposal all the time. Learning to harness the centring and calming power of the breath is a really incredible way of changing the state of not just your mind but also your body and your physical sensations. It is one of the most powerful gateways to rebalance your nervous system, get out of fear-based thinking, break out of subconscious programmes and finally find the inner space to live a life of more ease and more calm.

Awakening to the power of the parasympathetic nervous system

My experience – along with the science we will explore in a moment – has shown me that we are not built for this constant activation and cannot be at our best if we don't have the rest-and-repair periods that we need to maintain a healthy mind and body.

All the elite athletes and teams I have worked with have always paid very close attention to the rest and recovery protocols and practices. They realised that, very often, the rest and recovery is as important as the training. We are built to be still and to be present for large periods of our time. Yet when it comes to the organisations and people I work with outside a sporting environment, it is as if the importance of rest and recovery is either not known or it is ignored. To a more worrying point in some organisations, they actually reward over-working and see never switching off as a badge of honour.

My work involves helping them realise that 'busy' is often the enemy of excellence, and 'fatigue' is the enemy of health and performance.

Let's take a quick look at some of the important and simple science behind this. The autonomic nervous system regulates the internal physiological processes we don't consciously think about (i.e. respiration, cardiac regulation and reflexes). Divided into the sympathetic nervous system ('fight or flight') and parasympathetic nervous system ('rest and digest'), this system maintains homeostasis within the body and does a good job of keeping us alive and functioning.

In this section, I will focus on and describe the role of the sympathetic and the parasympathetic parts, as they are really important in understanding why living in an always-on, always-distracted mode can have a very negative impact on our physical and mental health and well-being.

The sympathetic nervous system

The sympathetic nervous system directs the body's rapid response to dangerous or stressful situations. It stimulates the adrenal glands, triggering the release of adrenaline and noradrenaline, putting us into a state known as fight or flight. A number of changes happen to our body when we are in fight-or-flight mode, including increased heart rate, increased blood pressure, increased breathing rate and a decrease in digestion.

This burst of hormones boosts the body's alertness and heart rate, sending extra blood to the muscles. In a short-term, emergency situation this is exactly what we need to give us the heightened energy and alertness we require to overcome the immediate threat or challenge causing the stress.

However, we must also realise that if we spend a prolonged time in the sympathetic, dominant stress state, the stress signals being fired around the brain and body will have a real and negative impact on our health and well-being. Spending long periods of our day in this sympathetic, dominant state means that we maintain constant mental stress, which we call chronic stress. The prolonged exposure to the hormones of stress, such as adrenaline and cortisol, actually damages blood vessels, increases blood pressure, promotes a build-up of fat and slows down (and even stops) digestion.

In fact, we know from science that chronic stress negatively disrupts almost every system in our bodies. It can suppress your immune system and cause imbalances in your digestive and reproductive systems, it will increase the risk of heart attack and stroke, and will speed up the ageing process.

Very often we treat these symptoms independently, without actually removing the ongoing or underlying stress, which means the root cause will still persist and eventually lead to greater sickness because we are not treating the symptoms. The most worrying part is that this chronic stress has unfortunately become the norm for so many, so that it has begun to feel normal.

The parasympathetic nervous system

The parasympathetic nervous system is responsible for the body's relaxation, its rest and digestion response and abilities. It is what allows your body and mind to rest and recover, especially after you experience elevated emotion or physical stress.

It has an incredible ability to reset and rebalance your entire system by decreasing respiration and heart rate and increasing digestion, among other functions.

Learning to activate your parasympathetic nervous system is one of the best and most important health skills and abilities you can develop. Believe it or not, there are many powerful ways you can do this and most are very simple, free and you can use them anywhere and anytime.

One of the best and most accessible ways is breathing. Breathing exercises can help activate the parasympathetic. Science shows us that deep breathing – diaphragmatic breathing or belly breathing – increases the activity of the vagus nerve, which is a key part of the parasympathetic nervous system and controls the activity of many of our internal organs. Most of us are actually breathing far too fast and far too shallowly.

When we breathe in this fast and shallow state, it actually activates our sympathetic nervous system, while slowing and deepening our breath takes us out of sympathetic and into parasympathetic. The challenge for most people is to become present long enough to become aware of and change their breathing technique.

There are many other ways we can activate our parasympathetic nervous system, such as yoga or meditation, and we know that the food we eat plays an important role in keeping our nervous system balanced and healthy. Green leafy vegetables are rich in Vitamin B complex, Vitamin C, Vitamin E and magnesium, all of which are important for proper functioning of our nervous system.

We can wrongly associate 'busy' with 'productive'

This awakening to the power of our nervous system and the role of both the sympathetic and the parasympathetic systems was a massive changing point in my life. I realised that I had spent far too much of my time chasing goals, quickly moving from one task to another, working late into the night and up early the next morning.

Somewhere in my subconscious, I believed that busy was good and that being busy was somehow linked to being productive, which I saw as a huge part of my identity. A good day was a day I got loads done and I believed that resting, taking time off or taking time to do nothing was, in fact, a waste of my precious time.

After discovering the importance of the parasympathetic

nervous system and the importance of balancing our nervous system to become and to stay healthy, I started to give myself permission to build more rest and recovery into my lifestyle. I gave myself permission to exercise less and rest more, and

> 'We can wrongly associate "busy" with "productive" and, even more sadly, equate our self-esteem with our productivity.'

I realised that all exercise and all gym sessions did not have to be sessions where I pushed myself to the limit of exhaustion. I realised that very often the best exercise sessions were the ones that restored order and balance to my nervous system and that enabled me to lower the stress hormones in my system and replace them with more healthy and calming hormones.

I began to explore and practise yoga. At the start, I was so conditioned to exercise having to be hard and punishing that I told myself that yoga was too slow and too gentle. It wasn't until I had committed to really giving it ago, and not letting my ego or my fears stop me, that I realised that yoga was the part of my exercise routine that had been missing all my life.

Balancing our nervous system is one of the most important and powerful things we can do to protect our physical and mental health, and the more we educate ourselves around it and the more we do it and the more we realise we have to do it from an integrated perspective, the more our thoughts, nutrition, movement, breathing and sleep are improved. It's one of the biggest discoveries I have made.

In today's world of busyness, noise and distraction, our health is being challenged like never before. It could be said that one of the biggest obstacles to our health and happiness is the disease of distraction, this always-on culture that seems not only to encourage but reward those who live in that way.

We can wrongly associate 'busy' with 'productive' and, even more sadly, equate our self-esteem with our productivity.

A lack of ease in the mind can contribute to disease in the body

In many parts of the world, we are witnessing an incredible rise in chronic diseases and lifestyle-related ill-health and sickness – such as obesity, Type 2 diabetes, auto-immunity, digestive disorders, anxiety and depression – and very often we don't even stop to ask why this is happening on a fundamental level. We simply treat them as if they are inevitable and never really ask what is driving these rising numbers.

Many of these illnesses have a direct connection to the amount of daily stress we are under and the way in which we live our lives. My experience and research have led me to believe that one of the biggest root causes of unhappiness and ill-health is simply that we are living at a pace that we cannot sustain, a pace that is exhausting us and leading us into ill-health. Is it possible that we are actually thinking, working, eating and living ourselves into sickness?

As explained in Chapter 7, when we live in this constantly distracted way, it triggers us into fight-or-flight mode. This is a very specific state of arousal where we experience heightened emotional, physiological, psychological and chemical functioning when we feel threatened – be it a real or imagined threat. In short bursts, this is not a bad thing but in a longer, more sustained manner, it has many negative impacts.

The brain and the body find it hard to distinguish between threat and fatigue, so they respond to both in the same way. It can be a once-off physical threat that is outside of you or it can be an ongoing threat that is going on in your mind. In this perpetually distracted, over-aroused, over-activated state, we place ourselves in a state of chronic stress and this creates a host of physiological responses that are harmful to both our minds and bodies. This distracted state is a perfect breeding ground for worry and anxiety.

'My experience and research have led me to believe that one of the biggest root causes of unhappiness and ill-health is simply that we are living at a pace that we cannot sustain, a pace that is exhausting us and leading us into ill-health.'

For me, the human mind–body connection is very important, where we recognise that all the various mental, emotional, chemical and physiological systems are actually one integrated system, with all parts working together and where everything that one part of the system does affects and impacts all the others. Your mind includes your thoughts, beliefs, attitudes and emotions, and research has proven that various mental states positively or negatively affect our biological functioning. This is because the nervous, endocrine and immune systems all share a common chemical language, which enables constant communication and responses between the mind and body through important and specific messengers like hormones and neurotransmitters.

Our neurological pathways, which are what we ignite or 'fire' when we think or talk about something, connect the parts of the brain that process emotions with the spinal cord, the muscles, the cardiovascular system and our digestive system. This means that our very thoughts and words all have an impact on many of our biological functions. Our thoughts literally are sent all around our bodies.

Now we begin to see the truth about how our thoughts and emotions can impact our physical health. The reality that all our vital systems are interconnected affirms the incredible mind–body connection that influences the maintenance of health or the development of disease. Our thoughts and emotions have a direct impact on our health and immunity, on a biochemical, cellular and physiological level.

The beliefs, thoughts and emotions we hold internally are not just the driving force behind our actions but are at the very centre of our wellness or our sickness. Physically and chemically, our thoughts and emotions drive our wellness or our illness by flooding our systems with hormones and neurotransmitters like cortisol, serotonin and dopamine. While very helpful in small doses, these hormones and neurotransmitters become corrosive and destructive if not regulated.

'Many of us need to ask the question whether we are hyperventilating or suffocating in our own lives and is it time to stop, pause, reflect and breathe.'

There is one final piece that we must remember and take note of. All of our thoughts and emotions also carry vibrations. Different thoughts and words carry different vibrational

ARE YOU HYPERVENTILATING AND SUFFOCATING IN YOUR OWN LIFE?

It is important that we pause at the start and end of each breath. Pausing gives rhythm, depth and flow. Breathing requires three main parts.

1. The inhale: We take in the new.
2. The exhale: We let go of the old, that which no longer serves us.
3. The pause: At the beginning and end of each breath there is a natural pause. The pause separates one breath from another. The pause gives our breath depth and tuning. If you have ever tried breathing without a pause, where you are literally inhaling and exhaling as fast as you can, you will quickly realise that you are either hyperventilating or suffocating. The pause helps us to breathe in a healthy and sustainable way.

Many of us need to ask the question whether we are hyperventilating or suffocating in our own lives and is it time to stop, pause, reflect and breathe.

frequencies. These vibrational frequencies will either connect with and complement your body's natural, healthy vibrational frequency or they will disrupt it, and knock your natural frequency out of its normal resonance.

We call a healthy and connected resonance 'coherence'. Coherence is when all the main centres of the body are working together. The opposite is 'incoherence', whereby our systems are not working together and are sending conflicting messages to each other. In a state of incoherence, your body is forced to 'upregulate' those biological and physiological responses and genes associated with threat survival and, at the same time, 'downregulate' responses and genes associated with relaxation, digestion and healing.

At a physical level, we know the body is made up of atoms and water. Quantum physics has proven that these atoms are in a constant state of motion or vibration. After all, quantum physics proves that everything in our universe is energy at its very core, and energy is constantly moving in waves or vibrations.

This movement or frequency at which atoms within a cell vibrate creates a wave energy that will influence and change both the structure and the function of the cell.

So now we know that if your thoughts and emotions create a vibrational frequency, and a vibrational frequency can change the very structure and function of your cells, then you can begin to realise the power of your thoughts and emotions and how they manifest in your physical body.

Positive, kind and inspiring thoughts and emotions vibrate in harmony with your cells, as they share a similar frequency. Emotions like anger, fear, guilt, anxiety, sadness, resentment, jealousy, depression and stress carry a different vibrational frequency and can cause vibrational incoherence and imbalance, which we know can cause disease.

If emotional experiences affect the physiology within your body, the reverse is equally powerful. Healthy movement and physical rebalancing have a direct impact on your emotional and cognitive function.

Dopamine and distraction

In this modern world, there is little space in our day to unplug, switch off and be alone in and with our thoughts. With jobs, emails, social media, messaging platforms and a plethora of news sites, there is always something outside our minds and, very often, outside our own lives, demanding our attention and filling our minds with other people's lives, agendas and views. Sometimes, these can be things like family life or household chores, but they are things that keep us busy and take our energy and focus to external things rather than giving us the time and space to slow down and go inwards to rest, nourish and repair our own self.

These can give you a false sense of connection, with a temporary and fleeting feeling of reward. The likes you get, the ping of a notification, are all carefully designed by technology companies to activate you and stimulate your brain to release chemicals. These chemicals influence your motivation and mood.

This is down to the release of a very powerful neurotransmitter called dopamine. When this is released, we feel good, we feel safe and comfortable, and we feel satisfied. However, this neurotransmitter is often short-lived, so it leaves us wanting more and more, which is why we can become addicted to our screens, staring into the abyss of social media looking for approval and appreciation – and this really only serves to distract us from what's going on in our actual reality.

If we are constantly looking to the outside world for ideas, opinions and insights, then we must realise that the ideas, opinions and insights we are getting are someone else's – and, because our minds are being filled with external noise, we rarely get to hear our own ideas, opinions and insights. Our inner voice is drowned out by the external noise of others and we lose connection with our inner truths, and end up chasing and following the truths of others.

But, of course, this new-age digital craze is not all bad. It provides an amazing service to the world and is powerful beyond belief when used correctly. However, it's important that we learn how to use and manage it correctly, and become aware of our attachment and association with it.

We need to focus on our internal need to be distracted

This is just the first step to managing and understanding distraction. The external distraction is just the beginning, the tip of the iceberg. The real learning and the real opportunity arises when we no longer focus on external distractions and, instead, focus on our internal need to be distracted. We need to look at the root cause that drives our need to be distracted. This is certainly a challenge and something we need to learn to manage but, at a deeper level, I believe there is something bigger that is driving our need to be distracted.

Understanding the root-cause approach

In life, like in medicine, we need to ask the right questions and ask them on a deeper level. Treating the symptom is where we take a headache tablet to ease the headache but don't ask or change the thing that causes the headache in the first place.

Treating the symptom often looks like treating the physical aspect but never looking deeper to the mental or the emotional aspect.

Imagine if there was a pill for not being able to detect danger. Would you take it? Without our ability to experience or detect danger, we would walk out in front of traffic, put our hands in the fire and do many other dangerous things. Switching off your ability to feel and sense danger does not remove the danger itself, and does not remove the damage that the danger will cause. It simply switches off and removes our ability to realise we are in danger, but the damage is still being done.

Let me ask the question again: If there was a pill to stop you sensing or experiencing danger, would you take it? The answer is absolutely not. The ability to sense danger is a vital piece of natural intelligence, a vital sensory experience that enables us to know that something isn't quite right and make the necessary changes to keep us safe.

Now, go back to the headache pill. The pill switches off your ability to sense and feel the pain, it stops your body's ability to communicate with you that something is wrong and needs to be changed. Without this vital information, you switch off the sensory experience but you leave the cause of the pain untreated and unchanged – and, if you don't make any changes, it's the same as leaving your hand in the fire because you can't feel the pain.

So many of our modern pills are simply designed to switch off the sensory information, they are like the fire brigade arriving at a burning building and simply turning off the fire alarms and leaving the fire still burning. Turning off the fire alarms won't help, the fire needs to be put out. If we simply turn off the symptoms, if we simply turn off vital signals of the body, it won't make a difference, our bodies will still become more and more sick.

Treating symptoms only is where we switch off our vital senses. It's where we see pain as a bad thing, to be avoided and ignored. The truth is that pain is a very helpful piece of information. The pain may be a very real physical experience or a very real physical symptom, but the root cause may in fact be mental, emotional or because of something in our lifestyles.

As human beings, we all want to have more 'ease' in our lives and less 'dis-ease'. I have witnessed the benefits of people adopting an integrated approach to their health and wellness, one that encompasses lifestyle as medicine for sustained peace of mind and well-being in the body.

This approach looks beyond just the physical manifestation of the problem to the wider context and to the person as a whole, including how the person is eating, drinking, thinking, sleeping and moving. How much stress they have in their lives, how much fun and laughter they experience, how healthy their relationships are (not just with others but with themselves), their career (does it feed their soul with a sense of purpose and passion?), and what their core beliefs about themselves are and about the world around them.

What is really the root cause of our inner need to be distracted?

One of the main reasons we are or need to be distracted from our lives is because, at some level, we feel like our lives are not good enough, not exciting enough or that something is missing. The social media world, and even many of our mainstream media outlets of TV, newspapers and magazines, can drive a narrative that we always need to be doing more, chasing more and having more. We can often perceive the illusion of other people's lives as perfect, leading us to perhaps fear that we are simply not enough. We may feel flawed or we may judge, shame and blame ourselves. This, then, forces us to look for approval, appreciation, respect and validation from the external world.

When we need this constant external distraction, this need for external gratification, it is often because we don't feel comfortable or at ease in our own lives, in our own skin, in our own souls. But external things can only give us temporary gratification at best, they cannot give us real nourishment.

There is a very big difference between gratification and nourishment. If you don't actually nourish yourself – your mind and your spirit – you are left starving at an emotional and spiritual level. When you create and experience an inner vacuum, you can become frightened, so you deflect outward, constantly craving more and more external stimulation.

'The more time we spend invested in the world outside of ourselves, the more the outside world – along with other people's lives and ideas – becomes the place where we live.'

The more time we spend invested in the world outside of ourselves, the more the outside world – along with other people's lives and ideas – becomes the place where we live. Then, this external, transient world becomes our transient home, and the more this becomes our reality, the more we become homeless souls living externally in other people's worlds and our own soul, our true self, becomes homeless.

We live in a world of homeless souls

If you look around you right now – on buses, trains, in coffee shops, in hairdressers, in shopping malls, at bus stations, pretty much everywhere – you will see a mass of 'home-less' souls. You will witness a cascade of human beings glued to screens trying to prove to the world that they matter, hoping to be heard and seen, so that they can attain some sort of validation to reassure themselves that their lives are worthy and meaningful.

In order to overcome this dis-ease of distraction, we have to become more present in our own lives, so we must create our own home for our own soul. In the next chapter, we will look at how we can both nourish and find a home for our souls.

The future doesn't just happen

It is being created by the things you focus on, the things you give your energy to and the decisions you make right now.

Ask yourself a question: If you continue to live the way you live, work the way you work, eat the way you eat and nothing changes, how does that look in ten years in terms of your physical health, your mental health, your relationships? If you continue to live the way you live, putting your time and energy into the things you currently put them into and prioritising the things you do, what happens to your dreams and ambitions? What happens to your health?

If your answer makes you happy and proud, then the good news is you don't need to change a thing. If, however, that future picture (or parts of it) does not inspire or make you proud, then you need to make a change. In Part 2 of this book, we will look at ways in which you can make changes to enable you to live the life you want and deserve.

TAKE A MOMENT

This 4-7-8 breathing technique introduced by Dr Andrew Weil MD, an American doctor who is a thought leader in the field of integrated medicine, is a wonderful breathing practice that enables your body to drop into the parasympathetic nervous system. This will help reduce the amount of stress you feel in your body and mind and will also aid the body in its healing and restorative processes for enhanced health and vitality.

- To begin, make sure you're comfortable, in a seated position. Place the tip of your tongue to the roof of your mouth, just behind your front teeth.
- Begin by taking a slow, deep breath in through the nose for the count of four. Send this breath down to your belly and let it rise. Imagine your belly blowing up like a balloon – very gently and soft.
- At the top of this breath, pause for a count of seven.
- Then slowly exhale through your mouth, pursing your lips and making a 'whoosh' sound for a count of eight.
- Repeat the cycle up to four times.

This breathing pattern aims to reduce stress and anxiety and create more inner calm.

PART 2

The Path to Your True Self

11

The soul is visible

In this chapter, we will address what the soul is, the fact that the soul is visible, and how and why the soul needs to be nourished.

One of the biggest and most important discoveries I have made is realising that the human soul is visible. For years, I thought the human soul was something that was intangible and invisible, something that we rarely encountered. The moment I realised that the human soul is neither intangible nor invisible, everything changed.

The human soul is something we experience every single day. It is something that is impossible not to notice on a number of levels. Every single time we come in contact with another human being, we experience and encounter their soul. We must also realise that just as we encounter another person's soul when we meet them, they also encounter ours in a very real and visible way.

To show that our soul is a visible reality, a visible, tangible and instantly recognisable reality, take a look at the picture below of a beautiful baby. The baby with his eyes wide open, with his beautiful smile and his remarkable facial expressions. Take a few moments to look at the picture and then, in your head or on paper, list what you see when you look at the picture.

It's easy to guess what most of you will see in this picture. We see laughter, curiosity, freedom, happiness, confidence, presence and love. The more we look at it, the more we see the personality and charisma of the baby. The deeper we look into the eyes, the more we see.

For almost twenty years, in the talks and workshops I host, I have been asking thousands of people a very simple question that awakens the reality of the human spirit. Sometimes, I use a picture of a baby; sometimes I use a picture of an elderly person, but always their eyes are alive, they have a smile that is bright, and a sense of adventure is written on their face. I ask the audience what they see and the answers are always the same:

laughter, curiosity, freedom, happiness, confidence, presence and love.

What is remarkable is that, in all this time and with all the people I have asked, the answer is always about non-physical traits. People never say they see skin, bone structure, pupils and hair follicles. It is amazing that nobody ever says what they see is simply the physical, the anatomy.

It's as if, in these pictures, there is something more powerful and more striking than the physical anatomy. There is something that instantly captures our imaginations and our attention. Call it charisma or personality or spirit, the truth is these things are not invisible, we see and experience them all the time. In fact, they are the very first things we see when we meet and encounter another human being. Every single one of us is unique, perfectly unique, and we are most perfect in our uniqueness. The more you try to be like someone else or to squeeze yourself into someone else's expectations, the more you begin to smother your incredible and beautiful soul.

In my opinion, your soul is the very essence of who you are, it is that inner spark that shines beyond the physical; your soul is the spiritual or energy part of you that gives life to all the physical parts of your being. Your soul is your spark of the infinite energy from which we are all made. Your soul is the part of you that returns to the universe after the physical body has died, as we know energy cannot be destroyed, it can only be moved. Your soul is the energy that gives you life, and the part of you that is connected to the energy field that gives the universe its life.

'**Your soul matters.**
Your soul is beautiful.'
Your soul comes alive when you feel most alive and most free because you are being your authentic self. Your soul is beautiful. It is yours. It is unique to you. In the same way we see beauty in a baby's soul, that beauty and goodness is there in you always. You simply need to recognise it and set it free. Your soul matters, your happiness matters. When you realise the importance of your soul in your health, wellness, love and in happiness, you will realise the importance of becoming spiritually nourished and awake.

Anorexia of the soul

Just as the things we notice first when we meet other people are not the physical things, we must realise that when we encounter other people, the first thing they see is our soul.

Now, imagine if I had a photograph of you. A photograph of you right now or a photograph of you captured over the past six months. If I put that photo in this book and you and every reader was to look closely at that photo, what would they see? Would they see a spirit that is alive and full of confidence? A spirit full of adventure, that is following and speaking their truth and living their dreams? Or would they see a spirit that is tired, stagnated or fading? Would they see a spirit that is suffocating and starving in its current life? Would they see a spirit that is loved by you?

There is an anorexia that exists that has nothing to do with food or body weight but that is just as destructive and life-inhibiting. It is an anorexia of the soul. If you are living a life that is not allowing your soul to come alive, if you are inhibiting your dreams and passions, suppressing your imagination and creativity, then you are actually starving your soul, and your spirit will become malnourished and depleted. I believe this suppression and starvation of our soul is one of the biggest causes of human sadness, suffering and disease in our modern world.

As my wife Miriam Hussey says, 'If we spend our life looking outside of ourselves for nourishment, we will live a life of constant hunger and malnutrition.'

To heal anorexia of the soul we must heal any broken relations or self-imposed hatred or anger we have with ourselves. The antidote to anorexia of the soul is the cultivation of a loving, harmonious relationship with yourself.

Try the following practices to help develop a more loving, compassionate relationship with yourself. A relationship that is built on genuine respect and care.

TAKE A MOMENT

Daily mirror work
Come to your mirror and plant your two feet firmly on the ground. Take a deep breath in and a nice slow exhale out.

Look into your eyes and repeat some daily affirmations, either in your mind or out loud, as you gaze into your eyes.

Be kind and gentle to yourself. Know you are doing your best with what you have and with what you know.

Every day is a new day. A day to start over. A day to be reborn. Start your day with some loving, kind words to yourself and this will help you on the journey to healing any internal brokenness or lack of self-love fragmentations.

Below are some sample affirmations that you could use:

- I am a kind person.
- I have beautiful eyes.
- I honour my caring heart.
- I love and respect myself.
- I am willing to love myself. I am willing to try.
- I am enough. I am worthy.
- Today is a new day. A day of miracles and blessings. New opportunities await me today. I am ready.
- I choose to heal. I choose to refrain from self-judgement or shame today. Today, I see only the love and blessings in myself.
- I will honour and respect my body today with wholesome, nourishing foods and beverages that allow me to feel energised, alive and healthy.

FILLING UP YOUR INTERNAL CUP WITH
PRIMARY-CARE NOURISHMENT

Welcome to the concept of primary versus secondary foods – a concept that my wife Miriam learned at the Institute for Integrative Nutrition.

If something in your life right now is out of balance, or some part of your lifestyle or your primary foods is not really fulfilling you, you can end up developing a hole in your soul (anorexia of the soul).

These primary foods can be things like: that hug from a loved one when you are feeling anxious, or the calm you feel after a long talk with a friend. It's getting a promotion at work or seeing your child walk for the first time. It's that walk in nature or curling up with a good book.

These primary foods can be categorised into four main pillars:

- **Relationships**: Do you surround yourself with people who inspire you and grow your humanity?
- **Career**: Are you in a job that energises you and that you are truly passionate about?
- **Physical activity**: Do you have regular movement and flow in your life?
- **Spirituality**: Do you allow time in your day to stop, breathe and unplug from the busyness of life?

When we are out of balance in any of our primary foods, we tend to be out of balance in our lives and can lean on external things like food, alcohol or excessive work (our secondary foods) to try and fill us up or soothe and numb any uncomfortable situations.

A hole or a void in our primary foods causes us to overindulge in our external 'secondary foods' or substances to try and compensate. However, no amount of external stuff will ever meet the need of an emotional hole or void deep within ourselves.

Primary foods satiate our hunger for life rather than our hunger for food.

Ask yourself in this moment:

- Do you have enough fun, laughter, joy, play and excitement in your life?
- Do you smile or laugh enough?
- Do you have loving relationships that nourish you on a soul level? Do these relationships bring you alive?
- Do you have a loving relationship with yourself?
- Are you passionate about what you do? Does your career ignite a spark of light or excitement in you? Are you enthusiastic about your job? Does it bring your soul alive?
- When was the last time you allowed yourself to feel a sense of freedom or liberation or adventure?

In order to heal anorexia of the soul we must begin to liberate the inner passion and lust for life that resides within. We must allow our soul to sing by giving ourselves permission to go after the things that our inner self is craving and calling us to do. If we continue to ignore or suppress our needs and our deepest desires – our 'primary foods' – then we will continue to harvest more anorexia of the soul.

- Make a list of your passions. What brings you alive? What do you love to do?
- Are you spending an adequate amount of time doing these things? Do you make time to fill up on these primary sources of nourishment?
- What small steps can you begin to take to enable you to prioritise these soulful activities?
- How can you enable your soul to come alive?

Amputated souls

We can lose many body parts and still survive, limbs can be amputated and we can still live a full and fulfilled life, but this is not the case with an amputated soul, which is by far the most debilitating of all human conditions and the saddest of all human losses.

We are all born with an inner knowing, an inner spirit, that knows who we are and what we dream of. Our spirit is our inner intelligence, our inner compass, and it knows how to both nourish and heal us. We are born with this amazing spirit of inner intelligence fully developed, fully alive and fully ignited. We do not have to earn it, deserve it or create it. It is a gift we inherit from birth.

As we will see in Chapter 14, we often, somewhere along our life journey, begin to doubt ourselves and we stop listening to our inner intelligence. We begin to suppress our soul. Very often, we suppress and deny our own truths in favour of the truths of others, we value social acceptance over self-expression, we limit and suppress ourselves so that we fit in because we are afraid to stand out for who we really are. We deny our soul its ability to express itself fully for fear of what others may think.

From that moment, we suppress the very thing that brings us fully alive, the very essence of who we are, and we bow to and settle for the person we think we should be – the person who will get us accepted by others. We settle for safety and security and deny passion and excitement, and we begin to create an inner hole, a void that will eventually become a hole in our soul, a weakening of our energy field.

External physical matters cannot fill an internal spiritual hole

My wife Miriam defines this even better: 'No external feed can meet an internal need.'

If we do not address this inner spiritual hole, this inner need or craving that we have, we will spend the rest of our lives consuming external matter in the form of work, food, social media, gambling and various other things in an attempt to fill this inner hole.

I believe that most addictions start with an inner hole in our souls and with a void that needs to be filled.

When we overconsume an external thing – be it work, social media, etc. – it can often be to suppress an emotion or meet an emotional need. These needs may include the need to be seen, to be heard, to be loved, to be in control or to avoid conflict. Sometimes, we consume external 'stuff' in an attempt to stimulate or invigorate a tired self or a tired soul. If you are bored, stressed, tired, angry and anxious on the inside, it can be far easier to run away from these emotions or avoid their root cause and instead go for a quick or easier fix on the outside.

Just as a coffee can be a quick and short-term solution for being tired, we also know that the only way we can really address fatigue is with rest and sleep. While the coffee may be a solution in the short term, in the end it will simply give way to and even magnify the original feeling or emotion.

In the same way, all external distractions, all external stimulants are things that may bring short-term stimulation or distraction but which, in the long term, cannot meet the real need of a soul that craves something far more powerful, like meaning, purpose, passion, self-belief, self-compassion and self-expression.

The word 'emotion' itself comes from the French émotion – via ex-movere (move out) and émouvoir (to excite). Another way I describe this is 'e-motion', energy in motion. So, the very basis of this means that our emotions are meant to be moved. If we don't allow our emotions to be expressed, felt, heard and moved, if we simply distract ourselves or suppress them with external stimulants, these undigested emotions will ensure that we become spiritually malnourished.

Over-consumption of material things is often a crutch we use to get a temporary release from the pain of desire –

> 'The relationship we have with our inner self, our inner thoughts and inner emotions is where the awakening happens and where real wellness starts and ends.'

a desire to scream, to speak up, to express an opinion, to leave a job or a relationship, or to be real and to be loved. Most adults in today's world are starving for things like fun, laughter, rest, play, adventure, freedom, love, connection, authenticity, compassion, self-care, spirituality, and need permission to pursue the things they truly desire.

If you are not living your life in alignment with your true passions, then it really doesn't matter how many green juices or kale salads you have. If your inner essence isn't ignited and motivated by love and desire, then you will eventually become tired, bored, frustrated, burned out or even sick. No amount of green juice can alkalise a toxic self-image.

Real and lasting wellness is not an external thing. Our personal wellness is not held by anybody or anything outside ourselves – it is held and caused by ourselves. Wellness is an internal relationship of self-discovery, awakening, encouragement and, above all, compassion. The relationship we have with our inner self, our inner thoughts and inner emotions is where the awakening happens and where real wellness starts and ends.

TAKE A MOMENT

To become more aware of your soul's desires and passions and to awaken to your truest and highest potential, ask yourself some really honest questions:

- Am I happy?
- Is my job/relationship/lifestyle complementing me and inspiring me?
- Do I connect with myself regularly through stillness, meditation and quiet time?
- Do I surround myself with people who want the best for me?
- Are my daily routines supporting the life I want to lead or are they inhibiting it?
- Am I in a relationship that truly nourishes me?
- Do I regularly spend time exploring and doing the things that set my heart on fire?
- Do I have fun and laugh often?
- Do I have people I can talk to when I feel scared, anxious or upset?
- Do I regularly move my body and exercise to release old, pent-up emotions?
- Do I have a spiritual practice that enables me to pray, meditate or unplug from the busyness of the world and enables me to practise some self-care?

If you can fill up your inside world with love and respect, you will be truly nourished, and the need to rely on material things will diminish and lose its potency.

Reflecting back on the time I was in the hospital, I now realise my soul was starving. I was trying to be what I thought others wanted me to be.

I was starving my inner spark of life, suffocating my own life force, my soul, and wondering why I felt so tired all the time and devoid of energy. I was not only neglecting the most powerful part of myself, I was actively shutting it off.

For too long, I had cursed my creative mind and my love of poetry and spirituality. I had also cursed the fact that I was no good at practical things, like woodwork, metalwork and maths. I had become so intent on proving that I could do these things that I became overly focused on them, trying to prove to myself that I wasn't stupid.

What I didn't realise was that I simply wasn't interested in these things and that that was absolutely OK. Just because everyone in my school loved these subjects didn't mean I had to, and just because I struggled in these subjects did not mean I was stupid – it just meant my passion and brilliance lay elsewhere. But I didn't know this at the time, and I judged myself on my scores, not my passions. I was shutting off the very part of myself that gave me life and passion.

In hospital, for the first time, I was beginning to realise something very important. If I was to begin to rebuild and experience a new energy, if I was to stop feeling tired and exhausted all the time, then I needed to start re-energising my soul, my real self. It was time to stop suppressing, to stop suffocating my deepest self. It was time to awaken and reignite my soul and my spiritual self.

I had to believe that life was actually too short for me not to ignite my soul and live the life that brought me passion, love and laughter, and that I had to finally stop denying and suppressing my dreams, my ambitions, my truths and my real self. It was time to heal the anorexia of my soul.

But the question was: Why didn't I realise this before? Why had it taken me so long to start looking in the right place and start asking the right questions? I have discovered an interesting thing about us humans: many of us stop one question short of a major breakthrough and we miss the miracle that is life.

TAKE A MOMENT

In order to feel content, at ease and at peace, I believe we must feel secure within ourselves and aligned to our soul's purpose or calling.

To come home to your soul on a daily basis, try the following:

1. *Conscious breathing and meditation*
Start your day with some slow, deep diaphragmatic breaths (belly breathing). This will enable your soul to come to know internal rest. Settle, breathe and relax your body. Let your breath become slow. Let your mind become calm. Let go of any attachment to any specific thoughts or expectations. There is no right or wrong way to do this. Release all judgement or anticipation and just allow yourself to be here in this moment with no agenda.

When you allow yourself to get to a space of inner stillness, just observe and surrender. This place can become your inner sanctuary. It is only in this place of inner silence or rest that you can hear the calling of your soul and thus make life decisions and build lifestyle habits that honour your soul's calling.

In your meditation ask yourself: What does my soul want me to do, be or say today? What is it that my soul is asking of me? What is my soul's gift? Why am I here?

What have I been placed here to do or be? What kindness can I show the world? How can I serve? How can my unique gifts be of service to the world?

2. *Honouring your soul's values*
If we live a life that is out of alignment with our core values, then we create an inner tug of war, an inner disconnect that causes us to feel ungrounded and homeless.

- Take a moment to write down your deepest core values.
- Is the life you are living right now honouring these core values?
- Are you in a job, relationship, home environment that reflects your soul's values?
- Are there any values that are currently dormant, perhaps, and need to be revised and reignited?
- What small steps could you make to implement and ensure that your life reflects your values?

By doing this, you can start to come home to your soul and find your anchor within.

12

We have many states of consciousness but we don't use most of them

Awakening to our different levels of consciousness

While studying for my undergraduate degree, I started reading books on our various levels of consciousness and the role that each plays. I discovered that we can move from one level to the other, sometimes intentionally and sometimes unintentionally. I began to realise that if I could change my consciousness and uncover and unlock my subconscious and self-created beliefs and programmes, I had a real opportunity to change the way I viewed and experienced both myself and the world around me. I was realising that by expanding my consciousness, I could finally move beyond my past and my fears to become my true self.

In this chapter, we will focus on three main states of consciousness:

1. subconscious
2. consciousness
3. pure consciousness.

Each has its own specific function and purpose. Each is really important, and I want to explain as simply as I can the power and importance of each state and how we can both access and reshape them.

I will start with the one we have all heard about, but maybe don't fully understand or know how we can begin to use it to its full potential.

1. The role of the subconscious mind

Your subconscious mind is committed to doing three connected things:

1. keeping you alive
2. maintaining a sense of the familiar (in psychology, this is called homeostasis)
3. making decisions quickly, using past memories and expectations.

The subconscious mind uses fast reflex decisions. It doesn't value stopping to assess and reflect on what is actually going on and what a new and better response might be. It is not interested in the best possible reaction – it's simply interested in not dying and sticking with the familiar.

Our subconscious programmes are what keep us in a self-perpetuating sense of a familiar and constructed vision of the world, of ourselves and of what's going to happen. To the subconscious mind, the familiar breeds trust, comfort and loyalty.

It simply wants to help you make a fast, familiar decision that enables it to fulfil its expectations and beliefs about you and the world.

In many ways, your subconscious programmes are like the autopilot flying a plane to a pre-decided location. The location is our subconscious beliefs and the pilot is our unconscious programmes that take the necessary actions and decisions to make the journey.

The subconscious programmes are hardwired, and often outdated, thinking and behavioural habits that are based on past experiences and are committed to ensuring our life arrives at the same pre-decided point regardless of the outside environment or the infinite number of places it could go.

With every experience you have in life – especially the highly emotive ones that involve fear, shame or guilt – you create conclusions about these events and situations, and store the messages that will guide your future actions and decisions should a similar situation arise again. If at some stage in your childhood, you felt or perceived that you were rejected by someone, this could have created an internal high-emotional response that you stored in your memory. If, at some later stage in your life, you experience a similar situation, your subconscious mind will quickly search your known past and memories for all the times you felt rejected and will quickly start to replay the same thinking and response that you had as a child. This will reactivate the fears or beliefs that you are somehow unworthy or undeserving.

The amazing thing is that even if we experience a situation that goes against our internal subconscious beliefs – for example, if you meet someone who finds you attractive and there is the possibility of starting a great relationship, but you believe they couldn't find you attractive or you believe that they wouldn't love the real you – we will manipulate and self-sabotage the situation to ensure the outcome fits our subconscious beliefs.

Our subconscious mind will happily reject and reframe any version of reality that doesn't fit its already created inner beliefs and memories. When the relationship fails to happen, or does happen but eventually fails, we will even tell ourselves, 'I knew that wasn't going to work'; our love life has just fallen victim to our deepest inner beliefs.

Your subconscious mind will work incredibly hard to convince you to go back to your old ways of behaving and thinking because it is terrified and resistant to change, particularly in high-emotive situations, though we must also remember that this doesn't just apply to these types of situations. Your subconscious mind is constantly downloading the decisions you make and the habits you have, even in everyday activities, and storing these as 'the way we do things' so that they become automatic. The route we take to work, the coffee we order, the television shows we watch, the side of the bed we sleep on, etc. – we build up a set of habits and often don't even know why, but we rarely go against them. Even thinking about changing them brings up a feeling of unease.

This is why, in certain situations, we tend to act in similar ways and get similar responses. Well, in many ways, the subconscious is the very thing that prevents us from doing things differently and it's happy if we keep getting the same result, even if it is not the result we want.

In committing to new ways of thinking, behaving and creating a new life vision, we will often have to overcome our subconscious mind. It will tell us all types of stories to get us to fall back into our familiar past. Stories like, 'You had a good week of nutrition and you went to the gym so, go on, you deserve a night of chocolate and wine', 'You went on a holiday with a loved one and you had loads of romantic walks that you loved but when you come home, you won't have time to put that effort in', 'You signed up for a charity 5K and loved training for it but now you don't need to keep up your running as you don't have a competition to train for'.

We need to break away from a state of conditioned habits and reflexes and achieve a state of conscious decision-making where we are free and able to make new choices to achieve a new reality. We need to break the cycle of our conditioned programmes and stories that are running in our minds. We need to change the record in order to hear a new song.

Subconscious beliefs

We see the world not as it is, but as we are.

As we have established, a building cannot stand outside the size of its foundations, and our lives cannot be bigger or better than the size of our inner beliefs.

I have come to realise that the limits of our world are very often only the limits of our subconscious beliefs. These beliefs are the pre-decided limits that our lives stay within and the pre-decided locations they end up occupying. In some ways, from an early age, we have already pre-decided the life we deserve, the dreams we are capable of achieving and the relationships we will have and deserve. When we have formed these predetermined beliefs, they become the destinations of all our life's pursuits – unless we change our subconscious beliefs.

Our brain operates in theta brainwave pattern for the first eight years of our lives. As mentioned in Chapter 2, theta brainwaves are how we assimilate and download information, so we can learn about the world quickly. Believe it or not, most of our adult beliefs about ourselves were built during this stage of our development.

Very often in life we are not actually responding to the situation that is unfolding in front of us, we are responding to our interpretation of what is happening, a subjective, selective version of reality and we are manipulating it to affirm and match our inner beliefs. All too often, our external world is simply an extension of our inner beliefs; we can become hypersensitive to the external things that match our inner picture and totally blind to everything else.

In psychology, this is called 'pattern matching'. It's a process by which the subconscious creates an inner picture based on a memory of a similar situation or your preconceived expectation of how you expect the situation to go. When your subconscious mind has created this inner picture, your conscious mind will scan your environment and select only the things that match your inner, already created picture, and it will ignore everything that doesn't. This often means you miss lots of details and information that are right in front of you and, instead, only select the pieces that match your inner beliefs and expectations. In fact, so much of your reality is actually a subjectively created version or interpretation of reality that serves and meets your own inner beliefs.

The next time someone says something you perceive as being an insult or a slight, take a moment to examine the situation. Was the comment directed at you personally? What emotional state was the person saying it in? Was their intention to hurt you or offend you – and where is this coming from? Are you taking the comment the wrong way because of how you are feeling that day?

How are our subconscious beliefs formed?

We can form inner beliefs in many ways. One is by internalising the voice or opinion of an external person and replaying it internally again and again. A second is by freezing an emotion from a certain time in our lives and allowing that emotion to replay over and over so that it eventually becomes our permanent inner emotional climate.

We experience the world through the
lens of our own subconscious beliefs

This inner, permanent voice or emotional climate becomes the one that is guiding, directing and controlling everything we see and experience, and every decision we make.

No matter how much our external world changes or expands, we can still only operate within the limits of these subconscious beliefs. No matter how much the external climate changes, we will still only experience it within the limits of our internal climate. Think of driving a car. If you have the heater on it doesn't matter what temperature it is on the outside of the car, all you will feel is the temperature you have set inside the car. Our inner subconscious climate is the same as the car. It's the one that is closest to us and the one in which we live and, regardless of how the external climate changes, until we change the settings on our inner heater, it will always stay the same temperature.

The good news is that just like the heater in the car, our subconscious beliefs can be adjusted and changed and when we do, we experience a totally different experience of life.

As mentioned, until the age of eight our brain is operating on a theta brainwave level. This brainwave enables us to absorb and store information rapidly and creates an understanding of ourselves and our universe. In this stage, we are literally downloading and recording everything, we are forming our beliefs and storing them securely in our subconscious beliefs and, once recorded, we will replay them over and over again throughout our lives. That is why, in my experience, most adults are living a life that is trying to meet the unmet emotional needs they had as an eight-year-old, or are still living within the limits of their self-belief that they formed at eight years old.

TAKE A MOMENT

- What are the beliefs you hold about yourself that are keeping you in the place you are?
- What are the beliefs you hold about yourself that are keeping you in a job you don't like?
- What are the beliefs you hold about yourself that are keeping you in a relationship that doesn't make you happy?

Subconscious expectations

Our subconscious expectations are a combination of our subconscious beliefs and programmes that have a bank of stored history of our experiences and how certain experiences and situations end. When we encounter these experiences and situations again, the mind can speed up the outcomes and quickly give us the exact outcome we had the last time we experienced it. We end up at exactly the same outcome as we did before because our mind simply put the new situation and the old situation in one box and gave us the same outcome.

The subconscious mind is always trying to give us the experiences and sensations that we expect. By giving us the experiences and sensations that we expect, we continue to live within the limits of the familiar and, the more familiar and predictable our experiences and sensations are, the safer the subconscious mind feels. After all, the role of the subconscious mind is to keep us safe; going outside of our predictable past is seen as unsafe and dangerous, so the subconscious mind will resist it.

To show our subconscious expectations in action in an everyday situation, think about the first cup of coffee you have in the morning or the first cup of tea. Maybe it's the coffee you have immediately after getting up, when you feel groggy and know that that coffee will help you wake up. Or maybe it's the coffee you have after you get up, get dressed and commute to work, and then just before you start your day, you take a few minutes for this simple pleasure. Either way, think about when you take that first sip of that lovely coffee, that first mouthful.

Immediately, your subconscious mind is experiencing the familiar mug, the familiar smell, the familiar sounds of it being made, the familiar temperature and the familiar taste of it as you drink. The interesting thing is to ask yourself how long after taking the first sip does it take before you start to feel better, before you start to think, *I needed that*. We all know the answer.

The truth is, most of us begin to feel better straight away. Most of us start to feel the effects of that nice, strong coffee seconds after we drink it. However, the important question is, how long does it take for caffeine to be in our system? The truth is it takes up to forty-five minutes for caffeine to be absorbed. It will be at least ten to fifteen minutes before the very first traces start to even enter our organs.

So, the interesting question is: How do we all feel the effect of coffee straightaway? The answer is simple. Your subconscious mind set up your subconscious expectations, as you had various coffees over the years. Each time, your subconscious mind learned that forty-five minutes after you drank the coffee, you would feel certain effects, and after feeling these same effects a number of times, they became associated or linked to the smell, tastes, temperature and even the sounds of the coffee being made. Now, all your subconscious mind requires is a number of these things and it will use them to fire your subconscious expectations and speed up the process.

It will give you the feeling that you had come to expect long before the caffeine hits your system. Because you rewarded the subconscious mind with the familiar, the predictable past, by choosing to drink the same coffee in the same way, it rewarded you for staying within the familiar past by releasing dopamine, which is a very powerful, feel-good neurotransmitter linked to reward.

So, your brain is actually chemically rewarding you for staying within the limits of the familiar past. The experience you have from drinking coffee has, in the first forty-five minutes, little to do with anything that is in the coffee and everything to do with what is going on in your subconscious and what is being released in your brain. It has everything to do with all the coffees you've ever drunk. You just paid for a coffee, but the nice feeling you got from drinking it was actually created initially by your brain, for free.

Subconscious expectations are very powerful and can help speed up how we experience the world. The danger is they can also control our behaviours and decisions. They can trap us in the familiar past and make us fearful of or resistant to change by manipulating our experiences from what they actually are into what we expect them to be.

Subconscious programmes

Our subconscious programmes are the thinking habits and mechanisms that the mind uses to fulfil our inner subconscious beliefs and expectations. Think of the subconscious programmes as the builders that build the building from the blueprint. The builders don't design the building or create the blueprint for it, they simply follow the plan and execute what is in the plan. Our subconscious beliefs are the blueprints, our subconscious programmes are the builders that are actively executing what is in the blueprint and bringing it from a design to a physical reality. They are busy filling in gaps, bending something new to look like something old, cutting up opportunities to fit into old beliefs and building walls around anything that threatens the subconscious beliefs and expectations.

To demonstrate the power of our subconscious programmes and how they can fill in gaps and bend and reshape new reality to create an old belief, take a look at the paragraph below and see what happens:

*It deosn't mttaer in waht oredr the ltteers in a wrod are, the
olny iprmoetnt tihng is taht the frist and lsat ltteer be at the
rghit pclae. The rset can be a toatl mses and you can sitll raed
it wouthit a porbelm. Tihs is bcuseae the huamn mnid deos
not raed ervey lteter by istlef, but the wrod as a wlohe.*

I bet, at first, you saw a load of jumbled-up letters and words
that made no sense and yet, in a very short time, they began to
make sense and you were able to read the paragraph. Without
knowing it, your subconscious mind was scanning the page and
using past memories to make sense of what it was looking at. It
used past memories of words you have previously read to create
a new paragraph. Your brain simply needs a rough outline, a
number of cues and then your subconscious mind instantly
fills in the gap using your past experiences, and will often fill in
the gaps to the point where we no longer see what is actually in
front of us.

But the truth is that the paragraph your mind created, the
paragraph you ended up reading, is not actually on the paper. It
is simply in your mind and in your past memory of words. Now
every time you look at this paragraph, your subconscious mind
will instantly superimpose the self-created paragraph over what's
actually written on the page.

Our brain doesn't like disorder, it doesn't like gaps, so it will
quickly fill in gaps and create a sense of order even if that doesn't
actually exist. Our brains will resist seeing what is actually there
and give us what it thinks should be there. Our brains have
the ability to use a known or familiar context from the past to

reorder what we experience in order to make fast predictions about what we are seeing and hearing and what is to come.

Your subconscious mind will actually resist going outside of evolving itself

To stop you going outside of your comfort zone, the subconscious mind will fill the unknown with all types of imagined threats. The subconscious mind will convince you that having new experiences, trying new things, arriving at new outcomes involves danger, and a high possibility of disappointment and regret. These are very powerful emotions that none of us want to feel and the subconscious mind knows that, so it creates an illusion of situations that may occur if we try something new and it convinces us that, if these situations did happen, we would feel disappointment and regret.

The scary thing is, you spend up to 95 per cent of your day operating from subconscious programmes and beliefs. In committing to new ways of thinking and behaving, you will often have to overcome your single biggest enemy in the face of change: your subconscious mind. It will tell you all types of stories to get you to fall back into your familiar past.

We need to break away from a state of conditioned reflexes and achieve a state of conscious decision-making that enables us to break out of the conditioned programmes, beliefs and expectations that are running in our subconscious minds. We need to change the record.

One of the key ways we can change our inner subconscious programmes is by becoming more conscious, by beginning to actually observe the things we say, the things we do, the things we eat, and how they impact us. We can start to ask better questions: Are these things actually helping me or inhibiting me? Are these things enabling me to be at my best? What are the daily habits that I am imprisoned by or addicted to?

By becoming more conscious, we are using a different part of the brain and awakening new ways of seeing both ourselves and the world.

2. Your conscious mind

We also have a conscious mind that is a far more present and, in many ways, important field of consciousness because it is in this state of consciousness that we have the ability to be present and see things as they actually are, and not a reflection of our past. To fully awaken our true and authentic self, and to see the full potential of the world and not simply the limits of our subconscious beliefs, we must awaken the conscious mind.

In this conscious mind, we shift into the prefrontal cortex of the brain and are no longer in the limbic part, no longer running on emotional stress and anxiety, and no longer running from subconscious preconditioned expectations, beliefs, reflexes and programmes.

When we switch from the subconscious mind into the conscious mind, we become present in the moment where we can not only better see what is happening in our outer world but also more clearly observe our inner thoughts, emotions and actions and ask ourselves if this is the best possible response for us to make.

When we become conscious of our thoughts, emotions and actions, we can ask a really important question: Is the way I am responding opening my mind or closing it? Is it opening my heart or closing it? We can then begin to consciously think about what a new or better response would look like.

TAKE A MOMENT

The practice of daily mindfulness enables us to get into the ultimate state of presence. To learn the art of being more present in life, try out these mindful practices:

1. *Box breathing*: Focus on your breath. Inhale to the count of four. Pause at the top of the inhale and hold this pause for four counts. Exhale for four counts and then pause again at the end of your exhale and hold it for four counts. Repeat this practice several times a day. It will help re-centre you, ground you and bring you back to the present moment.

2. *Mindful senses*: Regularly throughout your day take a few moments to check in with what is going on around you. Become mindful of the smells and scents around you. Take time to really smell your morning coffee. Use essential oils to calm your nervous system. Smell the fragrance of your hand soap, freshly cut grass, wild flowers, etc.

Become mindful of the sounds around you. Take a moment to just stop, pause and listen. Can you hear the birds singing? Can you hear a lawnmower in the distance? Maybe you hear the ocean? Children playing? Cars moving?

Become mindful of your sense of touch and bodily sensations. Do a body scan. Check in with how you are feeling physically. What sensations can you feel? With each and every sensation there is information.

The very act of focusing your awareness on certain things like smell, sound and other sensations takes you into a centred, focused place – called the present moment.

3. *W.I.N. – What's Important Now*: Use this mantra daily to help draw you back to the present moment and shift you out of subconscious programmes or mindless distraction.

    Ask yourself regularly: What am I giving energy to?

    Use this affirmation to bring you back to the present: 'I choose to be in the here and now. I have a choice and I choose to respond in a soulful, life-affirming way.'

4. *Heartbeats*: Place your hand on your heart and simply count ten heartbeats. This pause is an incredible way of connecting you to the powerhouse of your body – your heart. The beat of your heart is a great reminder that you are alive. A life-force energy. And a great way to bring you back to gratitude and back to the present moment.

5.   *Object-focused mindfulness*: Bring your gaze towards a point of focus (e.g. a candle burning, a flower, your cup of tea). Soften your gaze and keep your concentration on this object. You may notice that you become distracted, either by external noise or internal voices or busy thoughts. If so, know that this is completely normal, human and OK. Don't judge this or resist it. Just keep bringing your awareness back to the object and back into the present moment. This practice can be done anywhere and at any time. It can be done proactively to anchor yourself into your day or it can be done as a tool to bring you back if you find yourself getting overwhelmed, distressed or distracted throughout the day.

═══════════════════

Creating a gap between stimulus and response

The things and situations that we encounter in our outer world are the stimulus, and the way in which we interpret and respond mentally and emotionally to that stimulus is our response.

Consciousness enables us to create a gap between stimulus and response, and when we expand that gap, we are no longer operating as preconditioned reflexes. By creating a gap between stimulus and response, we create an opportunity to choose our response. It is in this gap between stimulus and response that our ability to grow and develop exists. The more we expand this gap, the less we are conditioned by reflexes and the more we grow our ability to be defined not by what happens to us but how we choose to respond. When working with elite athletes and clients, I focus on creating and widening the gap between stimulus and response – this is where the true power of the mind comes alive.

The challenge is that we only spend 5 per cent of our thinking time in the conscious mind. It is so important that we start to create habits and routines that enable us to become conscious far more often. Morning habits that allow us to wake up gently and allow us to gain inner calm and clarity, habits that allow us to focus on what we want and not what we fear, and morning habits that allow us to begin the day in the present moment and not in the past or the future.

We should also build in good habits around breathing. We have discussed the power of our breath already in Chapter 10 and provided some practical exercises throughout the book, and these should become part of your everyday habits. In Chapter 20 I will give you a number of important habits and techniques that I have used and still use to help me stay in the present moment, habits that enable me to choose my response regardless of what is happening around me, habits that enable me to act from a place of love and not fear and habits that enable me to create and maintain a healthy gap between the things I encounter, which is the stimulus, and my reaction, which is the response.

Creating and maintaining this gap between stimulus and response is one of the most important things we can do in order to stay consciously awake and consciously choosing the life we desire.

*We see the world not as it is, but
how our limited sensory ability allows*

We must still be aware that so much of what we experience in the conscious mind comes to us through our physical senses. This means that we experience so much of our world in the form of touch, sight, sound, smell or taste. What we may not know is that all of these senses use light and vibrations and everything that is external to us is taken in as a piece of sensory information that has to be ordered by our inner world.

The only things that exist in the universe are in fact energy and information, and what is mind-blowing is that so much of what we see and experience is actually what our minds have created using this energy and information.

For instance, there is no sound in the world, only vibrational frequency and energy. It is the mechanics of the ear that transform vibrational frequency into sound. Music is simply vibrational waves that are created in energy by the instrument and when the vibration is fast enough the ear turns this energetic vibration into sound. Without the ear, the world has no sound or at least sound as most of us experience it. We know that musicians with hearing loss can actually use the vibration of their instrument, or the surface to which it is connected, to help them feel and experience the sound that they are creating. Vibrations caused by musical sounds help them 'listen' to music through the vibrational frequency.

We must also recognise that other species have the ability to hear frequencies that we can't. This means that different species will experience the sound of the world in completely different ways. When the human can hear only silence, lots of other species – a dog, for example – can transfer that vibration into sound. Sound is a construct of our inner ear, it's a subjective construction and does not belong to the world but belongs to the person hearing it.

What is equally exciting is the fact that it is not just sound that is a construct of the individual, but many other things in the universe that we experience are too. Colour is another fascinating example. Colour does not actually exist in the world. It is entirely a creation of the inner brain. The brain has a complex system that interprets frequencies of reflected light as it bounces off objects and enters the eyes. When this frequency of light has entered the eye, it is then converted into electrochemical signals and sent through the optic nerve, where it is interpreted as the colour or the image we think we are seeing.

The most obvious example of this in action is the blue sky that we all see. What we all might not know is that the sky is not actually blue. The sky has no colour, the sky is comprised of colourless gases. Depending on your relative angle to the sun and the moisture content of the air as you look at the sky, you will experience the sky in different shades. Of course, these changing shades have nothing to do with the external sky and only relate to your inner interpretation of vibrational light as it passes through moisture. We superimpose colour onto the sky that does not actually exist in the sky – but if we are not aware of this fact, we can easily believe that the sky is blue. The same is true of the ocean.

This happens in so many other ways. Where the way we

see and experience an external object has little to do with the inherent nature or colour of the object but more to do with the equipment, and often limited equipment, of the human sensory system.

I am often asked how different people can see and experience the same thing in a very similar way if it is a subjective or internal construct. Well, the answer is simple: most of us humans share the exact same sensory processing equipment and therefore we are all limited in the same way. Think of a community of people that only have black-and-white televisions. They have never seen or heard of colour television, so they don't believe in it and because everyone they know has the same limited technology – everyone confirms each other's false bias. The only way they can ever experience colour television is by upgrading their television, their technology. In a similar way, we will only experience the world as it actually is if we change or upgrade the physical technology our body is using, which isn't always easy.

This is why I use a particular expression with all my clients: we see the world not as it is but as we are. Or another way of saying this is: we see the world not as it is but how our limited sensory ability allows.

But this is not a new fact or a new discovery. I first came across this concept when studying the work of French philosopher René Descartes, who believed that since all external information comes to us through the physical senses, then we should be aware that all of the human physical senses can be fooled and that human physical senses are not capable of experiencing the external world as it really is.

Descartes believed that we should apply a healthy level of doubt to everything we experience through the conscious, physical, sensory mind. We should always be aware that, at best, it is only our interpretation of what's actually out there. We must always be aware that our vision and experience of the world is ours, it's subjective. We should always ensure that our inner beliefs and viewpoints remain open to evolving as we gain new information.

The fact that we are conscious and can observe ourselves brings us to one of the most exciting and unanswered questions that still exists in medicine and neuroscience: Where does the part of you that is observing you exist?

We know it is not in the brain. We know the physical brain cannot feel emotion or pain and yet we know there is a strong part of us that does feel pain, shame, fear, guilt, passion, joy and love.

None of the sensory equipment that we have in the brain – none of its synapses, none of the billions of neuro-synaptic connections of the brain, none of the neurotransmitters, none of our bones or organs, none of our ligaments or tendons and none of our blood vessels or arteries – is capable of feeling any emotion. They are only capable of the level of consciousness that is required to feel these things, they are incapable of the level of consciousness that is required to observe you thinking, feeling and acting. All these are simply mechanical, biological and chemical processes.

We have to look elsewhere to understand where this observer level of you exists, we have to look to the pure conscious.

3. Pure consciousness

There is a higher level of consciousness that is by far our most powerful and most accurate state of being, feeling and manifesting. If we think of the old image of the iceberg that is used to show the difference between the conscious and subconscious mind, the top 10 per cent is the conscious mind and the part below the water, the largest part, is the subconscious mind.

Let's use this iceberg image to explain the next level of consciousness – pure consciousness. Pure consciousness is the sea that surrounds the iceberg. Without the sea, there is nothing to hold the iceberg, nothing to distinguish between the part above the water and the part below the water; in fact without water there is no sea and no iceberg. Without pure consciousness, there is no other consciousness.

Pure consciousness is where we go beyond what we are experiencing through the physical senses and awaken a level of insight and knowing that is deeper and often more accurate than our physical senses and our physical being. Pure consciousness is where we leave our own local memories and expectations, where we get beyond the noise of the physical sensory world, beyond the sensations of our physical body and we access the world that is beyond the physical.

By doing this, we can connect with the universal or unified field, which is the field that connects everything that is, it's a real and measurable energy field. Think of the unified field as the sea that surrounds the iceberg. When we do this, we get out of the lower vibrational frequency that is driven by our fears and anxiety, and connect to the vibrational frequency of the unified field – and when we do, we experience ease, grace, freedom and liberation.

When we access pure consciousness, we are no longer uploading inner and subconscious pictures onto the screen of life, we are actually downloading a whole new picture that is much clearer and much more powerful than anything we can create in our human minds.

Pure consciousness. This is where flow state happens. It is where we get out of our own memories and our own past experiences. Think of a baby in the womb. The mum and dad can do the best they can to help the baby develop – but the baby knows how to develop. There is something in the baby. There is some electrical charge that is enabling billions of brain neurons to form, enabling stem cells to become liver cells, lung cells, kidney cells. There is an incredible natural state of consciousness or field of intelligence that we are all connected to. So even when mum is asleep, the baby is receiving a signal, it's downloading from a blueprint somewhere and it's becoming the best expression of itself. At the moment, no doctor, no scientist can explain where this electrical signal, this consciousness, is coming from. That pure untapped consciousness has an incredible intelligence.

We can all re-access this incredible pure consciousness anytime we want with a little training and practice. Through exercises like meditation we can get out of the subconscious programmes, we can become conscious and then we can open the next door into pure consciousness and that is flow state.

In flow state, you instinctively know the right thing. You see things more quickly and with more clarity because you are no longer distracted by memories, fears or expectations. You are simply responding, downloading, from that natural intelligence. The most incredible songwriters and artists have created their best work when they were in the state of pure consciousness and were not even thinking consciously about it.

I work with people who have written the most incredible songs in twenty minutes, but they might have spent the two days before that meditating. When I ask some of the athletes I work with about moments during their greatest performance and what they were thinking about at the time, they will all say they weren't thinking of anything. It's almost like we need to stop chasing mind*ful*ness and instead explore mind*less*ness where we are actually free of conscious thought. The more we try to do something, the more we overthink something, the less likely we are to do it.

Flow state is when we leave our human experiences and all that is our constructed human self and we enter that which is eternal and infinite and is beyond physical, beyond human. When we are in this magnified field of pure consciousness we instinctively know, see, feel things in a whole different, clearer, more powerful way.

'Flow state is when we leave our human experiences and all that is our constructed human self and we enter that which is eternal and infinite and is beyond physical, beyond human.'

We can all tap into this. It is a universal field or, as the quantum physicists would call it, the quantum field. It has also been known as the magnified field or the unified field. It is simply the field from which there is a signal that enabled you to create your own body. Imagine that intelligence. The billions of fibres that have gone into creating you. There is a natural intelligence at play in this universal field that has created the whole universe, the rhythm of the stars in the sky and everything that is.

Every single one of us is a spiritual being. We are energy. We are quantum energy. This whole universe is a field of interconnected energy. We know that every single one of us is more energy than matter. When you allow the energy of the unified field, that universal energy, to flow through you, when you get out of your own subconscious programmes and let go of your past, get out of your own thoughts, you become one with everything that is and begin to experience a total feeling of connection and completion.

When you realise that you are an energy field connected to this infinite source energy field, you realise that the same power that moves oceans is available to you. You realise that you are not a robot or some type of separate being looking at nature and looking at the universe, you realise that, in fact, you are nature and you are part of this incredible universe. You realise that you are the universe looking back on itself.

Sometimes, I will put a chair in front of a group of people I'm speaking to and put a number of dumbbells on it, maybe five weighing twenty-five kilogrammes. The audience watches me load the chair with weights and I make sure I am making it look heavy.

I then ask three priming questions:

- Who goes to the gym every day? A few hands go up.
- Who goes to the gym every day and lifts weights? Very few hands go up.
- Who'd like to make a show of themselves in front of people? Everybody starts laughing and no hands go up.

Then I ask, 'Who thinks they can lift this chair?'

No hands go up.

Then I say: 'Let me change everything by changing nothing. The chair still has 125 kilogrammes on it – but your three-year-old daughter is trapped under the chair. There's nobody else in the building. She will suffocate and will die in ten seconds unless you can lift the chair three inches. Do you think you can lift it now?'

Every hand goes up.

This is because now they are tapped into something else, out of fear and into love – because there is no distraction. We have to think beyond physical. We are spiritual beings having a physical experience. But we're not physical beings. We are more energy than matter.

Another really important question is: What would the chair have to weigh before you wouldn't even attempt to lift it if your child was trapped under it?

We all know the answer – no matter what it weighed, we would try to lift it if someone we loved was trapped underneath. Now, apply that same logic to your life.

What in your life right now are you not even trying? What if you could tap into that love and non-distraction and you were free from fear, where you didn't worry about what others might think and you let go of self-inhibiting thoughts and beliefs and you were now free to physically and mentally do your best for yourself? What could you achieve then? What's the life you could live?

Getting out of your own way

Neuroscience is an incredible field of study, teaching us incredible things about our physical brains. It has shown us so many great things that we need to know about the brain, but neuroscience struggles to find out where consciousness exists. We know the brain receives an electrical signal, it processes the electrical signal and it communicates the electrical signal, but nobody knows where the electrical signal comes from.

Consciousness does not lie in the brain.

I think when you can start to embrace that fact, you realise that we are energy fields, we have a magnetic field around us all the time and that your mind is not in your brain but your body is actually in your mind. Now you are beginning to see a whole new picture of your ability and potential.

Your brain is responding to your mind, and when you fill that mind with freedom and connection, to love and to self, when you get out of fear and you get out of your learned programmes and you get out of your own way, it is amazing what you can achieve. It is amazing the life that you can start to have for yourself.

Pure consciousness is where flow state happens. It is where I get out of my own memory and my own level of experience and I allow my body to do what it is naturally meant to do.

When you ask songwriters who have written the most incredible songs in minutes where their inspiration came from, they often have no idea. They will often say, 'It just came to me.'

The incredible question is: From where?

The field of pure consciousness is this universal field that connects every single thing that is in this created world. You can call this God or life force or the unified field or the quantum field.

To get access to this unified field of pure consciousness, we must leave all local identity descriptors and ego behind. We get access to the infinite, unified field of pure consciousness only when we release ourselves from the need to be defined by our physical, our past and our personal stories. We must release ourselves from our ego which is constantly using huge amounts of energy and resources to try and keep us as independent, separate beings. The ego does this because the fragile ego, born of the local world, is terrified that without that sense of separateness, without that sense of what makes us separate and different, we cease to exist.

This is the furthest thing from the truth. The truth is that when we access the universal field, when we surrender the need to be defined by labels and comparison, when we free ourselves from judgement and become part of the bigger field, we realise that we are all simply tiny pieces of an incredible masterpiece that is far bigger than we can ever possibly be by ourselves.

When we enter the universal field, we replace 'I am a teacher, a doctor, a mechanic, a mother'; we replace 'I am John, Mary'; we replace and surrender everything that would normally come after 'I am' – and we become comfortable in the simple expression, 'I am'.

Everything that comes after 'I am' is simply a tag, a label, a descriptor that belongs only to the physical, local world, and these labels are the tools of the fragile ego trying to convince us that we are separate, that we are being disconnected from everything else, that we are somehow our own universe. Everything that comes after 'I am' is simply a lessening of your true being.

Every single one of us is a spiritual being. We are energy. We are quantum energy. So, we know that every single one of us is more energy than matter.

Now we are getting really close to one of the most important questions: Who am I?

The more we look at the science, the more we awaken from fear and from subconscious beliefs, the more we move towards pure consciousness and the more we awaken to our authentic self, the more we realise it is here in the realm of pure consciousness that we discover what is perhaps the closest answer to the question: Who am I?

When we release all of the labels of the things we do and the things we have, maybe the most amazing fact is that the answer is simply: I am.

You are an energy field that is expressing itself in a physical form, but, all the while, the physical form is totally dependent on the energy field. When we change the frequency of our energy field, we change the way the physical matter manifests.

You are an energy field, a pure and infinite energy field connected to the unified field that has created and sustains everything. You are an infinite spiritual being having a physical experience.

When you allow that unified field, that universal energy, to flow through you, when you get out of your own subconscious programmes, get out of your past, get out of your own thoughts and become one with everything that is, you realise that the same power that moves oceans is available to you.

MEDITATION

Set aside ten or fifteen minutes to do this meditation.

To start: Come into a nice comfortable position. You can be seated or lying down. When you are ready, and feel comfortable, close your eyes and begin to turn your gaze inwards. Let's take a few moments to unplug from the outside world – a gentle reprieve from the external noise – and use this precious time to go inwards to hear your own voice of wisdom, to connect to your own life-giving breath and to come home to your heart. If you would prefer to keep your eyes open, that is also perfectly OK: you can just lower your gaze or bring your awareness to the tip of your nose, dropping the gaze softly and subtly towards the earth.

Relax your shoulders down and away from your ears and simply begin to soften the body. Start by releasing any tension or tightness from the muscles of your face. Notice any areas where you might be gripping, clenching or tightening. Let your jaw soften. Soften through the front and back of the neck. Let your temples be gentle and just begin to breathe.

Start by drawing air in through your nose and gently sending this breath down to the base of your belly, letting your belly rise and expand upwards and out like you are blowing up a balloon. At the top of this inhale there is a gentle pause. A beautiful space where peace resides. At the end of this pause there is a natural exhalation, and gently let your belly relax and fall, naval drawing back towards your spine.

Continue to breathe in this way for five or ten cycles – in and out of your nose, gently, slowly and softly. Feel the cool air entering through your nose, oxygenating your cells and purifying your mind. When you exhale, feel the subtle, warm air leave your body – taking with it any worries or fears that you may be harbouring today.

As you breathe in and out, imagine the lungs opening and expanding with this new life-force energy. Imagine this beautiful breath wrapping around your heart and fuelling it with infinite love, strength, power and passion. See your heart rising and expanding. Clearing and cleansing. Nurturing and soothing. Now that your heart space is open, ask yourself:

What would love do?

If you truly loved yourself, what is the life you would dream of? If you could overcome self-fear, what are the dreams you would pursue? If you cared less about what other people thought, what are the chances you would take?

Can you believe in you? Can you trust that this life is waiting for you to embrace it?

The universe wants you to be successful, the universe wants you to be happy.

The universe is ready and waiting to give you your dreams as soon as you believe in you.

As you continue to breathe in this way, let the following words wash over your body and settle into your heart

I am enough.

I am deserving. My dreams matter. My life matters.

I am enough.

I have always been enough.

I will always be enough.

To finish today's meditation, take three more deep, slow, cleansing breaths.

Come home to your heart, come home to your breath. Come home to your precious soul.

When you are ready, open your eyes and take a little stretch.

Well done.

13

We stop one question
short of a major breakthrough

I regularly speak to large crowds and sometimes I ask the audience a question: 'How many people here drive cars?' Hundreds of hands go up.

Then, I ask a second question: 'How many people here have been driving for more than ten years?' Again, hundreds of hands go up.

Then, I ask a third question: 'How do you make the car go faster?' Hundreds of hands go up, all certain they have the answer.

I ask a few people and their answer is always the same: 'To make the car go faster, you press the accelerator.' Everyone I ask thinks they have answered the question. However, they have not explained anything, they have simply described the process.

I then ask one more question because I believe most people stop one question short of a major breakthrough: 'Exactly what happens in the engine when you press the pedal and how does the pedal make that change?'

At this stage, most hands stay down and people are smiling. For years, we thought we had the answer but when we look a little more deeply, it no longer holds up or we realise we were not answering the question at all, we were simply describing the process.

The truth is far more incredible and inspiring than fiction

We are constantly surrounded by an infinite number of incredible happenings and reactions that are required to keep the earth moving and in perfect balance.

When you start to ask deeper questions about the universe, and not just about our planet but also our galaxy, you will be blown away by the incredible magnetic and electrical forces that are at play and how all of these principles and forces are equally applied to each of us. When we begin to realise the truth that everything in this created universe is actually energy and that space is never empty but full of energy and waves, and that this invisible a field of energy is what connects and creates everything, we begin to realise just how connected everything is, and this eliminates the inner feeling of being alone or being separate.

In a world where so many people feel alone, we need more than ever to realise that we are all part of a connected universe where each of us is part of the greater reality. In a world of lonely minds and hearts, all we have to do is open our soul to the reality of spiritual connection to all that is and embrace the immense masterpiece that is existence.

Without this incredible and invisible energy field, nothing would or could exist.

The truth about our universe is simply mind-blowing, and the truth about how little we actually understand is even more mind-blowing. In many ways, medicine can explain in detail what happens but doesn't actually understand how it happens. Doctors can describe in great detail how a foetus develops in the womb, but if you ask them to explain how the embryo knows exactly what week it is, or from where the embryo is downloading the programme to create the billions of cells and integrated, complex systems that it needs to put in place so that it can have a functioning brain, digestive system, muscular system, respiratory system, nervous system and all the internal organs, not to mention the billions of brain cells, doctors stop short of an explanation because, the truth is, we don't yet fully know.

When it comes to powerful questions – really powerful questions – the most powerful of all and the one most people simply don't know the real answer to is: Who am I?

Who am I?

It is singularly one of the most important questions and yet it is one we never seem to ask. I have always been fascinated with the obvious questions we never seem to ask.

Most people, in an attempt to answer this question, will rush into describing themselves in terms of their physical self, their jobs and the things they have. But, deep down, we know that these things do not actually define who we are, they are simply descriptions of the things we do, the roles we play or the things that have happened to us. Strip away all of that and ask someone to speak for sixty seconds about themselves but tell them they can't mention their jobs, their family or where they live, and most people run out of things to say after fifteen seconds.

The reason for this is that we tend to view ourselves through the roles we play and the things we do, we tend to define ourselves by our relationships to the things outside of us. This is because we can spend so much of our time focused on the importance and relevance of these things and we begin to believe that we are only relevant if we are relevant to them.

If we are relevant to our boss, to our friends, to our children, then we gain a feeling of relevance. Of course, there is nothing wrong with this, we are social beings and being relevant to a community is very important – but so too is our relevance to ourselves. We are not only important and relevant because we are needed and relevant to others outside of us, we must also become relevant to ourselves. In fact, until we become relevant and important, until our own health, our own dreams and our own lives become relevant to ourselves, we will live with this constant need to impress and meet the needs of everyone around us even if this means that we abandon ourselves.

When I see someone who is spending all their time and energy meeting the needs of others while abandoning their own needs, I ask them two simple questions:

• What is the belief you hold about yourself that is allowing you to abandon yourself?

- What is the belief you hold about yourself that is making you believe that everyone else is more important than you?

'We cannot become emotional slaves who believe that everyone is more important than we are.'

Abandoning your own needs, not being able to express your own needs and desires, is not too far away from being a slave. We cannot become emotional slaves who believe that everyone is more important than we are, and that our relevance and our importance is simply attached to what we do for others. We must also extend the same gift to ourselves and allow ourselves to become who we deserve to be.

In many ways, the biggest cause of our inner sadness and the biggest driver of our outer actions is the fact that we don't actually know who we are or, for some reason, we have created a version of ourselves that is far less than who we truly are or far less than we are really capable of becoming. By knowing who we really are, we can begin to focus more consciously on what we are actually here to do.

If you don't know who you are, you can easily spend your whole life doing things and chasing things that actually don't match, fulfil or nourish who you truly are and what you are here to do.

We can chase the wrong goals

When we build our identity on other people's expectations of us, we internalise those expectations from a very early age and we see our success as fulfilling these expectations even though they are not our own. If we don't learn to let go of others' expectations, we will spend our entire lives living with limits, chasing and trying to fulfil the expectations of others so we can be successful in their eyes.

At the beginning of this book, we spoke about letting go of the expectations of others and allowing yourself to be free from the pressure of external expectations and the pursuit of external affirmation. Now we will focus on the goals you are chasing and ask why.

There are questions I ask myself and my clients all the time. Questions that I think all of us will benefit from asking at least once in our lives:

- What goals are you chasing?
- Whose goals are they actually?
- Why are they the most important goals?

Sometimes, we listen to other people who tell us about the things that are important to them – important jobs, important ways to live. They can even tell us when to do these things, when we need to start thinking about buying a house, when we need to start a family, when we need to start thinking about retiring. The danger is if we don't apply our own personal filter to these comments, we will absorb the ideas, goals and dreams of those people as if they are our own.

We are exposed to all these ideas from a very early age. Parents and teachers tell us what good grades are, what good college courses are, and what good careers are. Think about the job you are working in. When and how did you decide to take this career path? For what reasons? Was this the job you dreamed of?

Financial security is a valid reason to take on any career, but people need to make sure they have enough of what feeds their soul in their lives to counterbalance material things. A job can meet our financial needs, but we also have to ask which of our needs it is not meeting. If it is not meeting your creative needs, if it is not igniting your passions, if it is not connected to your dreams, then you will end up with a healthy financial account, but your soul and your dreams could be bankrupt. If that is the case, the money will be little consolation if you arrive at the end of your life with money and little else.

Without a very strong and robust personal-life vision, or personal-life filter, we begin to internalise these beliefs and goals and, before we know it, we are chasing them and following a life path that is simply not ours. We are chasing the job that somebody else said was a 'good job', the promotion that someone else said was important – we can even end up chasing and staying with the partner that our family and friends say is right for us when, deep down, we really know they are not.

I often come across people who are in jobs that they don't really love, in careers that they are not passionate about and didn't ever dream about working in. I meet people who have dreams that have nothing to do with the career they are in, but the longer they stay in the career, the more their inner dreams get crushed and are eventually extinguished.

I meet people who are in jobs that don't stimulate them

and yet they choose to stay. I meet people who are in jobs and lifestyles that are actually making them sick and keeping them away from the people they love and yet, despite knowing and feeling this in a real and deep way, when I meet them they are pursuing a promotion, to give them more of the work they don't like, to spend even more hours away from the people they love and to further suppress and deny the life they actually dream of.

The questions we must ask ourselves are: Is this the job I dreamed about? Does this job bring my soul alive? Is this job holding me back in some way from the life I dreamed of? When and why did I decide to take and stay in this job? What is the belief I hold about myself that keeps me in this job?

We can also begin to look at the other goals and things we are pursuing in life and ask the same questions.

- What goals am I pursuing right now?
- Are they even my own goals?
- What did I dream of when I was eight years old?
- When did I stop thinking my own goals were possible?
- When did I stop thinking my own goals were important?

Before you put any more of your precious and limited time and energy into chasing your current goals, now is the time to stop and really re-evaluate and re-examine these goals.

Remember, we get 900 months in this life and we sleep 300 – which leaves us 600 months to live our precious life. Time is extremely short, and your goals are extremely important. Make sure that if you are chasing goals, they are yours, and make sure that it's your heart and soul that is creating them.

Goals can and do change as we do

As we grow up and change in life, it is perfectly normal for our goals to change too. Maybe you set a goal when you were nineteen or twenty, and now you are not that age anymore and not that person any more. It is not always the case that we have one goal that we spend our entire life chasing. Very often it is important to stop and ask: What's important now? Is this goal still relevant? Is it still nourishing me? Is it still important to me now?

Every cell in your body is constantly renewing and evolving, and so are you. It is important that you are not chasing the goals that are no longer relevant to you out of habit.

Take a moment to stop and breathe and listen to your inner voice. Ask yourself: Am I chasing the right life goals? Is there something else I would prefer?

Ask yourself: If I was fully confident and truly believed in myself, if I realised I only had 300 months to live, would I still chase these goals or would I change?

If the little voice inside is saying you would change, then hear it, honour it and allow yourself to ask the next question: Change to what?

When answering this question, allow yourself to dream without the limits of having to have a clear plan or the need to know every step. Allow yourself to dream with all your heart and answer another simple question: If you really loved yourself and really believed in yourself, what is your heart asking you to do? And know that your heart is never wrong.

———————

TAKE A MOMENT

A really powerful exercise to help you discover which goals are really important to you is to visit your ninety-eight-year-old self.

I often get my clients to do an extended guided meditation where they imagine that they are ninety-eight years old and living the last day of their life. I ask them to look back at their life and ask:

- What would you like people to say were your values?
- What were the dreams you would love to say you pursued?
- What types of people did you surround yourself with?
- What are the biggest lessons you learned in life?
- What made you most proud?
- What do you want people to say about you when you have died?
- What are the things you are glad you prioritised?
- What regrets do you have?

After reflecting back over your life, and based on your own inner dreams and desires, consider the following questions:

- What does success look like for you in your life?
- What are your soul and heart asking you to pursue?
- What would the cost of not pursuing these be?

Doing this exercise enables us to get out of the everyday noise and distraction and remind ourselves that life is short and precious and that we do have a choice, not just in how we are remembered, but in the things we prioritise and chase in life.

Start to create your own vision of success. A vision of success that is actually based on your vision for yourself and not a vision of success that is given to you from an external source.

Visiting our ninety-eight-year-old self

It can be very beneficial to begin to live our life with this new perspective and with the end in mind. The saddest part of getting to ninety-eight years old would be to look back on a life where you spent it chasing goals that weren't actually yours and ones that, when you got them, didn't actually make you happy – and then to realise that you left it too late to pursue the things that would have made you happy. Visit your ninety-eight-year-old self; they know what is truly in your heart and they have so much great advice that they are just waiting to give you.

All of this is so simple. Every time I host a workshop or a talk afterwards the most common thing that people say to me is: 'That's really powerful. It's amazing when you say it like that. It's amazing how short life is and how we chase the wrong goals and how little we really question, but it makes perfect sense when you think about it.'

My response is always the same. 'Yes, it makes sense when we think about it, the problem is most of us are not thinking.' What I mean is that most of us are so busy doing, so busy racing, that we seldom if ever take time to stop, reflect and ask ourselves the important questions. We are so busy trying to stay above the water in our everyday life that we seldom take time to stop and reflect and ask ourselves the bigger questions. In this type of life, we get caught up in the immediate but maybe not the important. We are so caught up attending to the immediate things, we never get a chance to stop, to reflect and to make the required changes to the important things.

There is an expression I use all the time: In order to manifest our dreams, in order to bring our intentions to life, we must align intention and attention.

Too many times we have inner dreams and plans, but they stay exactly as that, they stay inside us and are never manifested into our physical world. They become the dreams we only see when our eyes are closed, we become lost to the disease of distraction.

Create a vision for life, not a survival guide

If you are to manifest a life that is truly in alignment with your own dreams and ambitions, there are two things you must do.

Firstly, you must redefine what success actually looks like in your own life. You must define clearly what it is you really want in life and what success would look like at the end of your life. It must be a definition and a vision of success that is truly personal and truly yours and not something that someone else told you success would be.

Most businesses start with a vision, a very clear vision of what success looks like – in fact it is impossible to think of a business operating day to day, month to month without a clear vision, without a clear destination of where they want to go to guide and direct their decisions and actions. Yet many of us are living our lives, making day-to-day decisions and don't really have a vision of the life we want. Many of us are living lives where we are actually revolving and going around in circles and not actually evolving at all.

This is *your* one incredible life. It's short and it's very special and exciting and you and your dreams matter; this is not a dress rehearsal. Create a new and exciting vision, a clear picture of the things, the moments and the experiences you want your life to contain and then align your intention and attention and make sure that the pen that writes the story of your life is held firmly in your hand.

14

A new future starts by accessing the power of our thoughts

We are thinking, conscious beings, but are you thinking about and conscious of your thoughts and the power they have to liberate or imprison you?

It is estimated by psychologists that we have 70,000 to 80,000 thoughts in a day. I'm not sure who is counting, but I do know we have thousands and thousands of thoughts every single day, far more than many of us even realise. The problem with having so many thoughts on a daily basis, and getting so familiar with our inner stories, is that we almost don't pay any attention to them.

We get so used to having thoughts running through our minds that they go unchecked, unfiltered and unchallenged. This unfiltered, fast-flowing thought process helps in some ways as it enables us to do things quickly and without a lot of conscious energy. The problem with this is that our thoughts are far more than most of us think, and unless we learn to observe and check them, they have the ability to change and shape every aspect of our existence.

We also know that, despite the incredible number of thoughts we have, very few of them are directly related to the present moment. Our thoughts on any given day are about the past, the future and the present. Evidence is showing that we spend most of our time thinking about the past and the future, and very few of our thoughts are actually focused on the here and now.

The thoughts we have about the past usually deal with regret or hurt, and the ones we have about the future are usually filled with fear or anxiety. This anxiety may be caused by thinking about a threat that either no longer exists or was imagined and never actually existed at all.

So much of our time, our mental energy, is given to things that don't actually exist.

Thoughts can be liberating or imprisoning, healing or hurting

Thoughts are words. They are words that we already know. We never think in a foreign language that we don't understand. Every single thought we have has a specific meaning and causes a specific internal reaction. Thoughts are a very powerful tool of communication. The danger is that we often think that no one is listening to our thoughts and no one can hear them, and because we think no one is listening, we permit thoughts that are not helpful and can even be destructive and hurtful. We can say things to ourselves about ourselves that are not kind, that are not constructive and, most of the time, are not true.

We need to become conscious and aware of these habits, and recognise how many, or how few, of our thoughts are actually focused on the here and now. When we learn to switch off these past- and future-based thoughts, and let go of the emotions associated with them, we can begin to focus all our mental and emotional energy on the things that are actually happening right now, the things and people in this present moment.

When you learn to channel all your mental and emotional energy into the present moment and away from the past or future, you allow your brain, your fields of vision, your thinking capacity, your perspective to widen and expand, and your imagination and creativity to come alive. With this new way of thinking you can begin to see the world in a whole new light, you begin to see the power and opportunity in every moment.

Our lives go in the direction of the stories we tell ourselves

Our lives go in the direction of the stories we tell ourselves or, more accurately, in the direction of the stories we choose to believe. What are the stories you are telling yourself right now? Are they liberating or imprisoning or healing you? Or are they poisoning you?

Where did you create or hear the story you are listening to?

Very often when we become aware of the stories we are telling ourselves, we realise that they can be traced back to or connected to a specific time or person in our lives. We may have first heard them from an external source and then begun to internalise them and replay them over and over until eventually they became our own stories. We may have also created these inner stories.

In many ways it does not matter how or where you first got these stories and whether they are self-created stories or stories you have internalised from an external source, the most important thing is to recognise the subconscious stories you are running and replaying and to start to challenge them with some simple but important questions. We need to ask ourselves: What emotion is driving our inner stories? Is it compassion, self-acceptance and self-confidence? Or is it comparison, judgement, anger or fear?

The thoughts and stories that fill your mind may be different but, if you begin to see what the emotion or the belief is that is driving the story, then you can begin to see a habit and a pattern. This pattern shows you the thing you need to challenge and dissolve or change. Changing the emotion and belief that is driving your inner thoughts and stories is the starting point to changing how you experience the external world, how you respond to it. It is an important step in getting out of dysfunctional stories and allowing yourself to create new stories that are more in line with your authentic self and the life you want to experience.

Many of your thoughts are not true: separating fact from narrative

We need to be able to become aware of our inner thoughts and stories and be able to fact check them regularly. Our thoughts are not always true and, unless we take time to filter out the untrue ones, they will be all taken as true. The brain can easily entertain a thought that has absolutely no foundation or connection to reality.

We must be able to separate fact from narrative. Fact is an accurate representation of what is actually happening and is actually possible, while narrative is a manifestation and projection of emotion. If we are not careful, we can give all our time, energy and attention to the narrative that is absolutely not true, and very little energy and attention to the fact.

A simple starting point is to start fact-checking your thoughts. It is a simple and powerful way to begin to challenge old stories and thoughts, and replace them with new ones. We can't always stop negative thoughts from entering our minds, but success is having the ability to recognise them quickly and replace them. Fact-checking your inner stories is as simple as asking yourself:

- Are these inner stories actually true?
- Are they related to what's happening in the present or are they related to what I think happened in the past or what I think will happen in the future?
- Are my inner stories driven by fear or love?
- Are they about things I can control or things I can't control?
- Are they outcome- or process-focused?
- What would a better story sound like?

TAKE A MOMENT

Take a few minutes to answer the following reflective questions:

1. How good are you at noticing your emotional states? What clues you in to the fact that you are feeling one way or another?

2. Do you have a good emotional vocabulary? Where did you learn this? Can you express your emotions when needed?

3. How easy is it for you to tolerate your feelings? Are there some emotions that are easier for you to tolerate than others? Which ones?

4. Do you ever distract yourself or numb/suppress your emotions? Can you identify the triggers that cause these emotions or thinking responses? If so, what do you do or use to suppress these emotions? Do you use alcohol/food/cigarettes/work/drugs? What is the impact of this on your body, mind, mood and health?

5. Write down some practical steps towards recognising your emotions and releasing them in healthy ways.

6. Emotion is energy in motion. Each emotion needs to be moved out of the body. Name a few ways you can move your emotion out of your body on a daily basis.

Moving away from toxic self-talk

Do you sometimes say things to yourself about yourself that you wouldn't say to someone you love? Why?

If, at times, you say things to yourself about yourself that you wouldn't say to a child, then you need to stop and ask yourself what long-term impact this is having and will have.

The most important thing we need to remember is that there is always someone listening to our thoughts. And not just listening, but believing everything we say to ourselves about ourselves. Your subconscious mind is listening to everything you say to yourself and using these words to form its deepest beliefs about you and the world around you.

Your words are literally shaping your self-belief and, just as a building cannot stand outside the size of its foundation, you and your life can never be any bigger or better than the size and content of your beliefs.

The next time you are critical with yourself, the next time you say you can't do something or say that you could never do something, be aware that those very words are shaping your deepest inner beliefs and those inner beliefs will become your life experience.

Do you have an inner coach or an inner critic?

When you speak to yourself about yourself, you need to be mindful of whether the voice in your head is your inner coach or your inner critic – and what the impact of this is.

There is a very different impact and outcome depending on which one you are listening to. When you think of the way a great coach speaks to an athlete, the way the coach will encourage the athlete, build their confidence and quickly reframe failure, ask yourself if that is the way you speak to yourself. Or is the voice you have inside more committed to pointing out your faults and mistakes, and more committed to telling you all the reasons why something might not work? We all have to be committed to turning our inner voice from our inner critic into our inner coach.

Remind yourself who you are speaking to

The other person who is listening to everything you say is your eight-year-old self. We all hold our inner child inside and we need to be aware that everything we say, we are saying to that little child.

I get all my clients to get a photograph of themselves as a baby or as a young child and put it in their wallet. It was something I did myself that helped me challenge and change my inner critic. Then every time they become aware of the way they are speaking to themselves, they have to take out the picture and see how it feels to say those things to that child.

Imagine an eight-year-old child that spends hours painting a picture of a house for their mammy. They put all their heart and soul into it and fill it with love and colour, and are so excited about it. It's their interpretation of their house.

But, of course, eight-year-olds aren't always great artists and sometimes the colours are outside the lines and things are not quite how they are meant to be. Now imagine this eight-year-old child after spending hours painting their picture and being so proud and excited of it running into their mammy and giving it to her. Imagine if the mother's reaction was:

- The colours are outside the lines.
- The windows are in the wrong place.
- That doesn't look like our house.
- You should have painted something else.
- Your brother's picture is better.
- That was a waste of time.

Imagine the impact this would have on the child and imagine what it would do to their self-confidence and their love of painting. I bet even reading this you are thinking, What type of a person would say those things to a child? Well, maybe that type of person is you. Maybe you say these exact things to yourself and, when you do, your eight-year-old self is listening.

By permitting yourself to speak like this, you are doing the exact same thing to your own self. Your inner thoughts and words are impacting your self-confidence and passion. Now that you know your inner child is listening to everything you permit yourself to say, might you be willing to change your thoughts and inner stories?

We can actually think ourselves out of our dreams

I regularly ask clients when I meet them first a few very simple questions.

- Is this the life you dreamed about?
- When you were eight years old, what did you dream of working at and are you working at it?

Too many times when I ask these questions the answer to both questions is no. The sadder aspect is when I ask the next two questions.

- Why not?
- Who stopped you?

Then the realisation starts to dawn on them: nobody actually stopped them, nothing outside of themselves actually stopped them. The realisation is that it was themselves that stopped them, their inner stories and their inner thoughts. They lost confidence, they were afraid of failure, they told themselves it wouldn't work out, they told themselves that it was too risky, they simply told themselves a broken and untrue story enough times and they began to believe it. Having never fact checked it with anyone outside of themselves, their broken, untrue story became their outer truth.

The power of our inner stories and our inner thoughts is that we can actually think and self-talk ourselves out of our dreams and even think our way out without even going after them. Our very own dysfunctional inner stories, unchecked destructive thoughts and words we allow to run over and over again, are the ending point and the graveyard of most of our dreams.

The four voices in your head

I believe that we all have four main voices in our heads, though depending on the level of consciousness and the way we train our inner thoughts, certain voices become bigger, stronger and more listened to. The four voices are:

- the dreaming self
- the planning self
- the doubting self
- the quitting self.

The dreaming self

The dreaming self is the part of you that is connected to your inner dreams and it's always trying to get you to listen to and pay attention to those dreams. It reminds you that life is short and that the only person who can make your dreams come true is you.

The planning self

The planning self is the inner voice that listens to the dreaming self and begins to think of plans and ways of making your dreams a reality. Our planning self is simple and structured and very versatile and resourceful – when we give it time and space to express itself and its ideas.

The doubting self

The doubting self is the voice that has listened to all the negative, destructive and self-limiting things you have ever said to yourself about yourself, and has stored all of these things. When we contemplate change, the doubting self comes alive and starts to replay all these self-limiting thoughts. If we do not have a strong enough bank of self-affirming thoughts built up in our inner subconscious reserves, then these self-limiting thoughts will become the loudest and eventually the ones that are now directing our actions.

The quitting self

The quitting self is the final voice in our inner world, and it is driven by ego, fear and comparison. The quitting self is committed to two things: the familiar and the predictable. It will listen to everything that your doubting self says and quickly act on these self-limiting thoughts and stories and eventually, somehow, convince you to give up on your dreams.

It does this in subtle ways, telling us lies like: *The time isn't right, next week will be better; People who achieved the things I dream of are different or better than me; I don't have all the right resources or the full plan so I will wait.* The doubting self has an incredible way of making quitting sound like the right thing to do. It can even disguise quitting as waiting. So many people I have met are waiting for something before they begin to truly pursue their dreams, and the truth is, they don't even know what they are waiting for; in fact, they are not waiting at all, they are quitting.

If we are not careful, we will believe we are waiting and not quitting, but waiting with no real reason, waiting when we have such a very short time, waiting for someone else's approval or permission that will never come, waiting for any of these things is simply quitting in disguise.

We all need to observe our thoughts and inner stories and regularly ask ourselves which of the four voices we are allowing to determine our life decisions and actions. By changing the way we think, and what we say to ourselves about ourselves, to a more constructive and more powerful version, and by taking time to regularly acknowledge and honour our successes and wins, we are building a healthy bank of positive resources that will challenge our doubting self. So instead of the doubting self giving way to the quitting self, this new way of thinking, these new learned inner stories, will have the power to challenge and overcome the doubting self and return us quickly to the planning and dreaming self.

Thoughts trigger emotional and physical changes

We are now aware that every single thought drives an emotional response. What we know from Chapter 16 on the mind–body connection is that these emotions have a direct impact on our physiological and bio-chemical makeup, and that they set off a train of reactions not just in our minds but in our bodies.

Thoughts that are fear-based ignite the amygdala in the brain, which is at the centre of our limbic brain (our emotional centre), releasing stress chemicals into our system and putting our central nervous system into high alert. This means that our mood and emotions are actually controlled not so much by our external world, but by our thoughts and how we think about our environment. Certain words like 'crisis' and 'deadline' and 'presentation' trigger a stress response that prevent us from being at our best, so we can literally talk ourselves out of a successful interview, exam or opportunity.

Words like 'love', 'peace' and 'opportunity' trigger a totally different emotion and a totally different physiological and bio-chemical response. This is why with all the high-performance athletes I work with, we create very powerful self-talk routines that can instantly change focus, change their emotional mood, change the body experience. This enables them to open up their visual field, their peripheral vision, become more aware of their fine motor movements and replicate learned muscle memory. All of these things are decreased if they are in a stress state and so all these things are either decreased or increased by the very words and stories they are allowing to run through their minds.

Each thought we have puts us into an emotional space and that emotional space is either opening our prefrontal cortex (the conscious part of our brains) and is capable of problem solving, taking in, processing and recording new data and information, enabling us to think and respond in new ways, or it is closing our prefrontal cortex and putting us back into the limbic brain, which has us reliving old experiences, so we begin to think and act in the same way and eventually get the same old result.

We cannot create a new reality, a new life or a new opportunity if we are using old thinking and seeing the present moment through the lens of the past. Unless we are able to get out of the limbic brain, that is exactly what we will be condemned to – old stories imprison us in old realities. This is why it is so important that we use thoughts and stories that are focused on solutions, not problems, focused on what's controllable and not what's uncontrollable.

The thinking, feeling, doing cycle

It is important to note that just as our thoughts and emotions affect our physical, physiological and bio-chemical body, the opposite is also true: if we get trapped in or fixated on a thought or emotional pattern, it can be hard to think our way out.

Neuroscience is proving that it is very hard to think our way out of an emotion. But we can, in fact, use our bodies to help us move out of an emotion or negative thinking process. As the body begins to move and free itself, so too does the mind. Our bodies can be a very powerful way of changing our inner thoughts and emotions. As we activate and move our bodies in certain ways, we trigger the brain to release new chemicals into our bodies and these new chemicals enable us to begin to think and feel in a whole new way.

That is why I refer to the power of exercise and movement as the medicine of movement. Sometimes, in order to shift and move our minds, we need to shift and change our bodies and our physiology. It is a beautiful and simple connected system where one impacts the other.

Thoughts are vibrations and change our vibrational frequency

The human brain consists of a tight network of nerve cells. All these cells interact with one another and generate an electrical field. We can measure this electrical field with fairly simple medical equipment; understanding human brainwave activity is an area for research that is giving us an ever-increasing understanding of the power and significance of brainwaves and the nature of the electricity that is flowing through our brains at any given minute.

In fact, it is not just your brain; your whole body is an energy field, and any time you have felt the shock of static electricity or used a touch-sensitive screen, you've proven that you have an electric field. Your thoughts are an important part of this electric field. The measurable changes in the brain's electric field that we can observe are actually your thoughts as they race through your mind. Thoughts create and change our electrical/energy field and, depending on the nature of these thoughts, different parts of our brains light up in direct response to our thoughts and our thinking activity.

We know that, because they are electricity, our thoughts have a vibrational frequency. This can be felt and measured and this has an impact on our physical bodies. We also know that certain thoughts, certain words, have different vibrational frequencies that send different messages not just throughout our brains and our bodies but outside of the brain and outside of the body.

This has two impacts.

The first is that it changes the vibrational frequency in our own self, which can trigger healing and recovery. We can literally impact the way our genes turn on and off and express themselves simply by changing the electrical frequency.

A vibrational frequency of fear will trigger our bodies and our cells to react by deferring rest and recovery and entering a survival state, which we know in the long term has a direct and detrimental impact on our health.

Understanding that we can consciously change and control our frequency is something that most people struggle with, including myself at the start. But the more I have explored and listened to incredible minds discuss this, and have seen the amazing work being doing in the area of epigenetics, the more I realise it can no longer be dismissed. We need to pay close attention to the thoughts we are allowing to run through our minds, the impact that has on our vibrational frequency and the impact that frequency has on our bodies and even our genes.

The second reason we need to be aware of our energy and our frequency is because the human body is literally sending these vibrational frequencies out into the world around us, which is going to impact the way people in our environment feel. If we are creating a vibrational frequency that makes others feel anxious, negative or not good enough, then we can be sure that people who value positivity, calmness and confidence will not want to be around us as the energy of the connection will not be correct.

We tend to build a group of friends from people who share our vibrational frequency and, by doing so, we are trapping ourselves into the same vibrational state of being. And, as we are energy and vibration at our very core, nothing in our physical being, nothing in our physical world can change until we change our vibrational frequency.

Ask yourself what type of friends you would like to have, and then consider if you are putting out the kind of vibrational frequency that would attract that type of person.

If we are creating a vibrational frequency that makes others feel anxious, negative or not good enough, then we can be sure that people who value positivity, calmness and confidence will not want to be around us as the energy of the connection will not be correct.

Quantum mechanics explains and demonstrates how electrons and photons behave and interact. When we apply this understanding and these principles to our thoughts, it means that, like any other set of particles or source of energy, we are connected with the environment around us and we are having an impact on it. We are literally connected to and changing the energy field around us, which is, in part, creating the people and situations that we find around us – we are energetically attracting certain things and events into our lives and we are pushing others away. Changing our frequency is a massive part of changing not just what is going on inside us but also what is going on outside us.

Thoughts are energy, and what we know is that wherever energy flows, these things grow. Choose and observe your thoughts wisely because they have an impact on every single aspect of our lives.

> 'Thoughts are energy, and what we know is that wherever energy flows, these things grow. Choose and observe your thoughts wisely because they have an impact on every single aspect of our lives.'

15

Open yourself to the magic of miracles

We focus on the wrong things and we miss the magic and miracles

You wake up in the morning and the sun is just coming up, it's early and you are tired. While you were sleeping, the earth rotated at exactly the right speed of 67,000 miles an hour in exactly the right direction, guided by gravitational force.

While it was doing this, the moon moved billions of tons of water all around the earth to ensure that all the tides are moving perfectly. The right amount of water is being moved, at exactly the right speed, by the sun and the moon, which are working off different but connected and synchronised forces to ensure this careful and essential harmony is kept in perfect balance. The moon moves a little further every day on its orbital journey than the sun, and so the tides caused by the moon's gravity occur exactly fifty minutes later than the tides caused by the sun's gravitational pull. Both of these cosmic entities are working perfectly and in harmony.

Also, while all this is happening, the trees are creating oxygen through photosynthesis, a staggering process that requires key functions of quantum mechanics and one we are only beginning to understand fully. This incredible process is filling the universe with oxygen, which is being taken in by your lungs, and your bronchiole, which look exactly like the trees, are repeating an equally remarkable process and converting the oxygen into carbon dioxide. This carbon dioxide is then taken back by the trees. And billions of plants and life forms are coming alive somehow knowing exactly what time it is and what to do.

While all of this incredible, interconnected and vital process is unfolding, right in front of your eyes, you have got out of bed, stayed half asleep and are now in the kitchen giving out because there is no milk. So often, we miss the magic and mystery of the universe and instead focus our attention on the wrong things.

We live in an active cosmic dance of gravitational force and magnetic fields. Yet, with so many incredible things that we could marvel at and be in awe of, we often choose to ignore them and, instead, be consumed by something insignificant. An important part of beginning to understand who we truly are and the truth about our universe is to actually take time to stop and observe it, to really see how incredible the whole thing is and how we tend to take it all for granted so often.

Finding the extra in the ordinary

Just imagine if one of these steps did not happen. What if the earth did not rotate, if the moon and sun did not move the tides, if the trees did not create oxygen and if your lungs did not take in the oxygen and seamlessly convert it back to carbon dioxide so the trees could repeat the process? If one of these things, any of these vital steps, did not happen, our day, our life and our world would be in trouble.

They say we don't appreciate things until they are taken away, but that is not the way it has to be.

With a little more awareness and a little more consciousness, we can begin to appreciate every single day how incredible this existence is and how connected every single thing is. With a little more conscious awareness, we begin to see the extra in the ordinary and we realise there is extraordinary everywhere we look.

This gives us perspective and appreciation, which are so important in maintaining a healthy vision for and healthy experience of life. We can often get pulled down into a thinking and emotional rabbit hole. When we do, our world and our life become very narrow and very dark. Perspective, appreciation and wonder at the majestic and mesmerising nature of our world is an essential part of opening and awakening our minds and hearts to the truth of the universe and the truth of ourselves.

When we open our minds to the miracles around us, we realise that science and medicine have lots of incredible answers, but we also realise that there are so many answers they simply do not have. In many ways, when it comes to understanding the universe, the unified field, the existence and purpose of black holes, science is simply scratching the surface. Equally, there are lots of areas in which medicine is simply scratching the surface to understand how our incredible bodies and all the connected systems within our bodies work.

As mentioned earlier, one of the most baffling questions that science or medicine is unable to answer is: Where does consciousness exist? Where does that part of you that is aware that you are reading this book, the part of you that is aware you are thinking and the part of you that is aware you have emotions, exist? Science and medicine still have no idea. You are actually one of the mysteries of this universe.

What this realisation enables us to do is look at our world as the incredible mystery that it is and realise that there is so much wonder and mystery out there. It enables us to ask questions like: How do we know for sure the world won't stop spinning? How do we know our internal systems will keep working as they are? How do we know that, when we fall asleep, we will wake up? How do we even know that, right now, we are not dreaming? The truth is, we don't.

We make predictions based on the past, but the one thing science has shown us is that the unexpected does happen and that, regularly, science will prove its historic beliefs wrong.

If we don't know these things, why are we not all running around worrying that the earth will stop spinning and be afraid to fall asleep in case we don't wake up? The answer is, we have faith. We trust in some truth or order in the universe; it is our inner ability to trust and to have faith that enables us to continue to live in a world where we have so little control and so little actual understanding about why we are here and how we came to be here.

Maybe our inner faith is more powerful than we think. Maybe it is our inner faith in the universe that is the starting point for understanding and achieving a life of inner peace.

16

The incredible mind–body connection

Awakening to integrated mind–body medicine

The more I worked on my own – and the more I studied mental health and what contributes to positive mental health and what contributes to mental ill-health – the more my experiences and research affirmed that our entire system – our minds, our bodies, our hormones, our nutrition, our emotions and our thoughts – is connected. If I was going to change my mental health in a meaningful and lasting way, it would have to be done using an integrated approach involving mind, body and spirit.

To this day, I have continued to work on and maintain my mental health from an integrated perspective, and so do all my clients.

Science is now recognising the powerful connections through which our emotional, spiritual and behavioural elements can directly impact our physical health. Research investigating the science of mind–body medicine is finding that emotions and thought patterns contribute to imbalances within the physical body. These connections between what is going on in your mind, heart and gut, and what is happening in your body, form the psycho-emotional roots of health and disease.

Research is showing that different mental states can positively or negatively affect your biological functioning. The nervous, endocrine and immune systems share a common chemical language, which enables constant communication between the mind and body through messengers like hormones and neurotransmitters.

For example, neurological pathways connect parts of the brain that process emotions with the spinal cord, muscles, cardiovascular system and digestive tract. This enables major life events, stressors or emotions to trigger physical changes. Emotions like anxiety can trigger increased stress hormones like cortisol and adrenaline, which suppress the immune system. Over time, ongoing or chronic psychological stress can change the way the body functions at both a hormonal and immunologic level.

We have twelve paired nerves in our head, neck and brain that are called the cranial nerves. These nerves play a hugely important role in the regulation of so many of our bodily functions, such as hearing and balance, vision, eye movement and pupil reflex, face movement, taste, swallowing, neck movement, movement sensations and abdominal organs and abdominal regulation.

The vagus nerve is the tenth cranial nerve. It is part of the parasympathetic nervous system, which we now know from Chapter 10 is really important in activating the rest and repair activities of the mind and body. It carries an extensive and important range of signals from the digestive system and organs to the brain, and vice versa. The primary role of the vagus nerve is the regulation of the function of our internal organs and vital activities, such as digestion, breathing and heart rate, and many of our reflex actions, such as coughing, sneezing and swallowing.

A healthy vagus nerve is essential to the functioning of our mind and body and yet many of us know very little about it. Stimulation of the vagus nerve through deep breathing deactivates the fight-or-flight response of the sympathetic nervous system and enables the body to activate the parasympathetic nervous system which activates rest, digestion and healing.

A healthy mind and soul deserve a healthy body and a healthy body deserves a healthy mind and soul. Both your incredible body and mind are amazing creations that often baffle both science and medicine.

For most of us, our body is a finely tuned masterpiece of incredible connections and systems, and it is not until something goes wrong that we really appreciate its incredible ability. From the millions of neuro-synaptic connections in the brain, your heart that regulates and maintains an incredible and important rhythm, your lungs performing a symphony of processes that transform life-giving oxygen into carbon dioxide that enables the trees to keeps this incredible cycle flowing, your eyes that are constantly perceiving light and shapes, your ears that have an almost miraculous ability to transform

> 'A healthy mind and soul deserve a healthy body and a healthy body deserves a healthy mind and soul.'

vibrational frequency into sound, to the millions of chemical exchanges that are taking place at every minute of your life from the digestive enzymes that help you to turn food into energy, the neurotransmitters that regulate mood and motivation, the incredible pancreas that regulates insulin, to the amazing way your body can regulate its temperature with such accuracy, to your skin that is performing so many amazing functions at all times without us even knowing it – this mind-blowing list goes on and on.

Our bodies are a finely tuned orchestra of moving parts that are somehow working in complete rhythm and understanding of each other, and it is because of these mystifying processes that we get to breathe, to laugh, to love, to eat, to dance, to do everything.

In the case of an illness that we are born with, a body part we have lost, a body shape we no longer have, we must realise that each of us has a body that is unique and does contain magic. Very often, our perceived disability can simply be the part of our body we dismiss or don't like. When we open up to our ability and not solely our disability, we can begin to see how amazing our bodies are. By accepting and learning to love the body we have, we can begin to heal from a place of inner love and gratitude, and no longer be poisoned by self-rejection or dismissal of the body we have right now.

Far too often, we are hard on ourselves because we don't run fast enough, we get disappointed if we don't hit a certain time, when really we should be so grateful that we get to run at all. We can be so judgemental of our bodies in spite of the fact that they do so many incredible things for us every single day.

It is so important that we begin to be aware of our incredible bodies and the gift that they are. If we were to become more aware of this, if we were to see the internal workings of our bodies and see the impact the food we eat and the thoughts we think have on our inner organs, I believe we would take a more whole and integrated approach to the way we live.

A simple task of taking a few moments every day to visualise or meditate on the gift of our incredible bodies and how important they are to us would make such a difference in the decisions we make and the actions we take.

The sad part is that so many of us are so distracted that we never take the time to marvel at our incredible bodies. While all of these awesome processes are happening in our bodies, we are giving out because we have a few wrinkles or because our body isn't exactly the size or shape we want it to be; we are so busy giving out about the little and often insignificant parts of our bodies that we completely miss the incredible miracle that we are walking around in.

Our three brains

What may shock most people is the fact that we actually have three brains. If we want to become our true selves, we must recognise all three brains and work to keep them in harmony with each other. They are:

1.   our head brain
2.   our gut brain
3.   our heart brain.

The three brains are like an orchestra, with billions of neurons co-operating to produce a harmonious symphony – harnessing together an ever-changing network of neurons that are designed to work in harmony with each other.

1. Our head brain

The brain in your head is the central processing unit of your body and serves an important role in receiving, ordering and translating the content from your mind (your thoughts, feelings, attitudes, beliefs, memories and imagination) into complex patterns of nerve-cell firing and chemical release that activate behaviour and physical response. It is very soft in texture and is the central organ of the human nervous system.

Neuroplasticity is the brain's ability to change itself constantly by creating new neural pathways and losing those that are no longer used. Neuroplasticity is what we call the process of change that happens in our head brain because of certain things like our behaviour, our environment, what we look at and what we listen to. We must realise that our brain is constantly changing and growing, it is a living entity that is renewing all the time. Your head brain is only about 2 per cent of your body weight and yet it accounts for 20 per cent of the body's oxygen demand.

During such changes, the brain engages in synaptic pruning, which means it actually deletes the pathways and connections we are not using and that are no longer necessary or useful. It gives a whole new understanding to the expression 'use it or lose it'. If you don't activate certain pathways of your brain, the brain will start deleting them.

The brain also strengthens the ones it thinks are necessary. It only knows which ones are necessary by listening to your thoughts and responding to your habits and actions. The human brain is capable of lifelong neuroplasticity and neurogenesis, which is its ability to regenerate and recreate new cells.

TAKE A MOMENT

Many people find it difficult to sustain a thought and to cognitively focus on one single thing for a sustained period. To achieve this sustained thought we need to generate or fire a single thought which will fire a brain neuron, then we fire another, related, thought which fires a connected neuron, and so on. As the signal from our neurons travels from one to another we create a neurological pathway. The more similar neurons we can fire, the longer we can sustain that thought and extend that pathway.

Sometimes what happens to our thoughts is that they lose direction and change pathways. Think of this as driving along a motorway and you are travelling in a certain direction using a certain lane. As long as you stay in that lane driving in that direction you will end up at the destination at the end of that motorway. Now imagine if you suddenly went onto the other side of the motorway and started driving in the opposite direction. Now you are on a different journey and you will end at a different destination. Think of your neurological pathways as the lane in the motorway. As long as you keep thinking in the same direction with the same emotion, then you are going to arrive at a certain destination. But if you change lane, change your neurological pathway, then your thinking is now going in a different direction and you are most likely thinking yourself away from where you actually want to be.

If we have a thought – such as, *I'd like to open a new business*, the next thought might be: *But now is not the time for that*. Then our pathway goes from opening a new business to firing in a completely different direction and we start to think about why we shouldn't open a new business. We know that if we change the direction of our thought, we change the neurological pathway.

The second reason we lose our train of thought is due to the presence of a different emotion. We might say we want to start a new business and then we get an emotion of fear. Fear actually has the ability to change the electrical circuit, the electrical current going to the brain. The fear then drives this in a whole new way.

Two things happen when we try to sustain the thought. We have the initial thought – *I'd like to start a new business* – and that starts to move along a pathway. Then we allow a second thought to come in and the second thought brings us in the opposite direction or a different direction. In addition, we have an emotion and we change emotion from excitement to fear and the fear shifts the neurological circuit or the electric current.

So, practise sustaining thoughts. A thought is something that lasts for a number of seconds and it needs to be backed up with another one, and another one, and another one. The more we do that, the more we fire the pathway, then the more we extend that pathway. Imagine you are standing on the shore of a river and the river is a hundred metres wide. You have a piece of timber that is ten metres long. So, you have to stand on that piece of timber, then another one, and another one, and make your way across using ten pieces of timber to get to the other side.

So, we do the same with our thoughts. Find a place that's nice and comfortable, and when you're in a nice calm position of focus or excitement, or a suitable emotion to attach to that thought, then have your first thought.

The first thought may be: *I am going to open my own business.*

Then we're going to have a similar second thought: *The business is going to be beautiful.*

Then follow up with a third thought: *The business will enable me to work in my own time and in my own way.*

Then have a fourth thought: *The business will enable me to turn my passion into my profession.*

Leave a second or two between each thought, each statement. Come up with ten consecutive statements. Each statement is going to fire ten consecutive thoughts on a similar pathway and see how many times you can get across before you lose focus. If you can fire ten in a row – fantastic.

Imagine you walk around and you start at the bank of the river again and you go across. So pick any statement – *I am healthy*; next, *I'm healthy because I feel good*; next, *I feel good because I had exercise today.*

It could be thoughts around our health, it could be thoughts of letting go of something that has annoyed us. The first thought is: *I'm letting go of that argument I had with my wife*. The second thought is: *She is my wife and I love her*. The third statement may be: *What we argued about was silly anyway*. Now, I'm working myself across the river.

This is what I do with Olympic champions. The first thought is: *I will be an Olympic champion*. The second thought is: *I will be Olympic champion because I've put the work in*. The third thought will be: *I will be Olympic champion because I've put the work in and I'm extremely talented*. The fourth thought may be: *I'm going to be Olympic champion because I've put the work in, I'm extremely talented and I believe in myself more than I have ever done before*.

If they can continue in the construction of ten thoughts that lead in the direction of the brain, they're spending an extended amount of time creating a neurological pathway to the brain, shaping a new belief and building the infrastructure in their brain that they need for that.

Before you start this exercise, get into a comfortable space, relax and think of your opening statement. Have your ten statements prepared. Imagine yourself on the shore of the river and you have to get across.

Try to state your ten consecutive statements nice and slowly with a pause of two or three seconds between each statement. Make sure that each statement adds to the positivity, adds to the focus and has the same intent as the next one. Of course, if you get to two or three thoughts and you get distracted, don't worry – come back and start again.

This is a really simple but powerful drill to build a new neurological pathway and to understand that we can be as focused as we want and that we don't have to get distracted every second or third thought. We have to be able to fire a neurological pathway in the direction that we want and, through our intent, keep that pathway firing along each neuron to create a longer path.

---

2. Our incredible gut brain and the gut–brain axis

The gut is often described as our second brain. We have just explored the vagus nerve and the role it plays linking the brain to the gut and its role in digestion and gut regulation. Now, let's look a little deeper at this incredible gut–brain connection.

The gut–brain axis, which includes our vagus nerve, connects the gastrointestinal system, the nervous system and the immune system with a vast array of cellular and biochemical messengers throughout the body, including the microbiome, hormones, cytokines and neurotransmitters. What may be most surprising to many is that the information travels mostly from the gut to the brain, rather than vice versa. This incredible and two-way communication system between our brains and our guts is called the gut–brain axis and it refers to the physical and chemical connections between your gut and your brain. Recent studies show us that your brain can affect your gut health and your gut can in turn affect your brain health and functioning.

An unbalanced or distressed intestine can send distress signals to your head brain and a distressed head brain can send signals directly to the gut. Therefore, a person's stomach or intestinal distress can be the cause of things such as anxiety and stress, and is even being linked to depression. That's because the brain and the gastrointestinal system are intimately connected. The gastrointestinal tract is very sensitive to emotion.

What goes into your body directly impacts your mind and your mental health. What we eat has the power to prevent or help reverse mental-health challenges. Specific nutrients have been linked to measurable positive outcomes in mental and emotional well-being. In addition, the mind–body connection comes alive in the constant and two-way communication between the brain and the gut. Researchers have found that people with healthy, diverse gut microbes are less likely to suffer from anxiety and depression.

Science is also showing us that some neurotransmitters are actually produced in the gut and not in the brain in our heads. Serotonin, which is referred to as our 'happy hormone' and is one of the primary hormones involved in mood and emotion regulation. The greatest concentration of serotonin (90 per cent) is found in the gastrointestinal tract with the remainder of the body's serotonin found in platelets and the central nervous system.

This means that so much of our mood and our happiness levels are actually determined and controlled not by the brain in our head but by our second brain, our gut.

This new information from science and medicine is reaffirming what the ancient wisdom teachings have somehow known for years. Hippocrates said around 400 BCE: 'Let thy food be thy medicine and medicine be thy food.'

This shows that, somehow, we have always known the importance of nutrition in preventing or curing disease and the importance of our gut to our immunity. Therefore if your gut and your brain are connected and one can impact upon the other, then surely the way that we treat our gut, through the foods that we ingest and lifestyle that we lead, can not only massively impact our digestion but also hugely impact our immunity as well as our mood and cognitive function, further impacting how we think and feel and the level of clarity and concentration we experience.

Anger, anxiety, sadness and elation can all trigger symptoms that are manifested and felt in our gut. The brain has a direct effect on the stomach and intestines. For example, the very thought of eating can release the stomach's juices before food is touched.

The brain–gut axis also explains how you can feel stress and emotions in your gut. Most people have experienced butterflies before a first date or before public speaking; we know these 'gut feelings' are the result of stress and it is a simple and practical example of the way our emotions impact and change the regulation and function of our gut.

3. The truth about our incredible hearts

For far too long, we have seen the heart as nothing more than a mechanical pump with one simple function: to pump blood around the body.

Science now shows us that our heart is far more powerful, performing so many more critical functions than we ever imagined. Your heart emits an electrical field sixty times greater in amplitude than the activity in your brain and an electromagnetic field 5,000 times stronger than that of the brain. The heart's magnetic field is the strongest field produced by the human body.

The heart has its own pacemakers independent of the brain. As long as it has oxygen, it will continue to beat. The heart could actually be removed from the body, placed in saline solution, given oxygen and still continue to beat. So even though the brain may be dead, the heart could continue to beat.

Heart intelligence can be described as a flow of awareness, an understanding and a level of intuition you experience when your mind and emotions are in a coherent alignment with your heart.

Andrew Armour has written incredible books on this topic and one I found fascinating is *Neurocardiology*. The work of Armour introduced me to this term and to the concept of the 'heart brain', where he explores the understanding that the heart possesses a complex and intrinsic nervous system that is a brain.

Beginning to think about our health and fitness in a new and more powerful, integrated way

The relevance of this science is that it opens up a whole new, more integrated and more powerful approach to health and fitness. Mental fitness is not just in our heads, and has a direct impact on our health and our ability to:

- be present with loved ones
- concentrate with ease
- switch off and find inner peace
- stay healthy
- maintain and build self-confidence
- think clearly under pressure
- make good decisions in line with our dreams, ambitions and life goals
- reframe and respond positively to adversity
- build and maintain inner resilience
- form meaningful and healthy relationships.

Mental fitness

Mental fitness impacts almost every aspect of our health and wellness, from our gut health to cell repair and recovery, to our mood, motivation and decision-making. Our mental fitness also impacts how we perceive, interpret and respond to our environment, so it's true to say that enhancing and upgrading your mental fitness can and will have a profound impact on many aspects of your life. Most people may not know that mental fitness is not only something you can develop and increase, but is something that actually requires and involves much more than the brain in our heads.

The work I was doing to release myself from the past, to let go of old hurts and dysfunctional stories

> 'Mental fitness impacts almost every aspect of our health and wellness, from our gut health to cell repair and recovery, to our mood, motivation and decision-making.'

and become more present and more at ease in my own life, was the start and now that I was experiencing the power of mental health and fitness, the next step was about how I maintained it. Mental health and fitness are things we need to consistently work on and maintain. Doing the work to achieve it is the first part, doing the work to maintain it is equally important.

Throughout my childhood, I thought there was something wrong with my brain and my mind. I wished I was born with a different brain and a different mind, and I felt imprisoned into thinking and living at the mercy of my current brain and mind for the rest of my life. It was like I believed my brain was a hardwired reality that was unchangeable and I was to simply accept it and live my entire life with it in its current form and abilities. I believed we were born with a brain that did certain things, was good at certain things and was not good at certain things.

I believed we were born with brains that made some of us confident and others not confident, some of us successful, and others not successful. I believed it was some type of genetic lottery and if you were born with the right type of gifted brain, you'd be destined for success, and if you were born with a brain that was not hardwired for success, then you would not be. I believed if you were born with a brain that was prewired to be happy and relaxed, then you would be exactly that, and if you were born with a brain that was hardwired for sadness and anxiety, then you were destined for exactly that.

Of course, I knew nothing about the brain back then. As I began to discover the real facts of the human brain, I realised that all the things I thought I knew, all the things that most people accept as true, were indeed completely false.

Of course, I didn't know at the time that, in fact, our brains are living organisms with an amazing ability to change and renew all the time. I didn't realise that I could actually retrain, upgrade and renew my brain, and make it into the brain I wanted. I didn't know then that the brain and the mind were not the same thing. I foolishly put them under the same umbrella and never really asked the right questions.

There are so many simple and powerful practices and exercises that we can do to help us maintain a healthy mental fitness and balanced interaction between the body, mind and spirit, including:

- yoga
- pranayama and mindful breathing practices
- tai chi
- guided imagery.

We now must waken to the realisation that true health and wellness, true vitality, needs to nourish and heal all these aspects of our being and that, if we exclude one from the healing process, we can never fully or truly heal.

In order to become our authentic self, we must first become our best and most healthy self.

17

Where we attach our energy and focus is where our future flows

A lesson in attachment: noodles at 30,000 feet

After the success of the Irish boxing team that I was working with at the 2008 Olympic Games, I was asked to work with a sports team that I had never met personally and in a sport that I wasn't familiar with. Before making a decision, I asked if I could go to a competition in advance and observe the team perform to get to know a little bit more about them and the sport.

I went to the next competition, which happened to be a world cup, and had a great chance to see how the athletes prepared and performed in pressurised environments. In the team, there was one particular athlete who was new to both the sport and the team. Although new to the sport, he had already shown phenomenal physical ability and had everybody very excited by his potential. What I noticed about him was that the closer we got to competition day, the more he became a little withdrawn and quiet.

I wasn't officially working with the team and there is little you can change so close to a competition, so I simply observed him.

On the day of competition, he was even quieter. Just before his race, he became fully aware of the packed arena, the noise, the television cameras in front of his face and, I am sure, he was very aware that his family were watching. I observed his body language as tension began to appear – his breathing rate increased and I tried to imagine what was running through his mind as he sat there with the packed arena and his family watching.

The time came and he went on the track. Very quickly after his race began, it became clear that the performance that we had hoped and he was capable of was not happening. Technically, he just wasn't racing correctly and he didn't seem to have the same explosive power physically that we had seen in all his training events. Quickly, the performance went from bad to worse and, before he knew it, the event and the opportunity that he had worked so hard for were gone.

Of course, he was devastated and couldn't really explain what had happened. I knew from the little I had seen that he had a real desire to win and real potential, so I agreed to work with him and the team to unlock what had happened so we could change it.

The next day we were on the flight home. I was thinking about how I could start to work with this kid and how I could help him understand what had happened – without first understanding something, it is hard to change it in a meaningful and lasting way. He was sitting in the aisle across from me and, before I knew it, my opportunity appeared. The inflight dinners had just been served and he was sitting eating his dinner while watching a movie.

He was clearly enjoying both the movie and the noodle dinner as his body language was relaxed, he was laughing, and breathing deeply and calmly.

This was an exceptional learning opportunity, so I sat beside him and briefly interrupted his movie to ask a few simple questions. I asked him how he was feeling. Of course, he said he was very disappointed and embarrassed about his performance the previous day. I then asked him how he was feeling right now. He said he was feeling better, feeling OK. I asked him how he had felt and how his mind had felt just before his competition, just before he was called onto the track. He told me his body felt tight, his heart was racing, his legs felt tired for some reason and he was very anxious. Understandable, maybe.

Then, I asked him to compare that feeling before his event to how he felt right now sitting here in this aircraft watching this movie and eating his noodle dinner. He said he felt far more relaxed now, his body was more relaxed, his mind was more relaxed, and his heart rate was much lower and he was much more centred.

I asked him then if he thought that it was unusual that he was sitting here in the aircraft feeling so relaxed and so calm when yesterday he felt so anxious. He was, of course, a little puzzled by my question. He said of course he felt more anxious yesterday and that he was under more pressure, with the packed arena, the cameras and all the distractions around him and all the things that could go wrong if he didn't perform.

I then reminded him that we were sitting in an aircraft which is a metal tube and we were 30,000 feet in the air. I expanded and reminded him that there were thousands of gallons of explosive fuel each side of us, sitting right beside the red-hot engines. His eyes opened up and he was beginning to see where I was going. I also reminded him that the plane was being flown by somebody he had never met and if at any given minute something went wrong we would most likely not survive.

I told him that I found it amazing that he could sit there, in the middle of all that danger and uncertainty, and yet be so relaxed and so calm. I asked him how he was able to do it. Now his eyes were wide open, and his body shifted; he had realised something really important. He had just realised that it's not actually our environment that makes us feel fearful, but it is the parts of the environment we are focusing on, it's the things we are attaching our energy to that creates our response. As we have the ability to choose what we attach our energy to, we also get to choose our emotion.

His answer was that he felt so relaxed on the flight because he was just focusing on the film and his dinner. By attaching all his focus and energy onto those things, he was able to ignore everything else. I asked him then if he thought it would be possible to apply the same logic in a sporting situation and, of course, he agreed absolutely.

For the next year, we worked closely together on his mindset, his focus ability and his distraction control ability. I trained him how to be in any environment and to focus only on the pieces that he wanted to focus on and ignore everything else. We worked on his ability to stay in the moment and stay present and attached only to the things that brought him reassurance and confidence, only the things that he could control.

One year later, we were back at the same competition, in the same environment, the same arena with all the same outer distractions. This time, he was sitting trackside and I observed him again. He was sitting calmly, breathing deeply and slowly, his body was relaxed and there was a smile on his face. I walked up to him just before he went on track, just before the biggest event of his sporting life; he saw me and smiled. I asked him how he felt.

He said, 'I'm feeling amazing. I am eating noodles at 30,000 feet and I feel amazing.'

Shortly after that, he won his country's first world-cup medal in that sport.

We all have the ability to choose the things in our environment that we give our attention to, we all have the ability to choose the things in our environment that we become energetically connected to. There will always be things in our environment that may cause stress or anxiety or fear, and there are always things in our environment – big things or little things – that if we choose to focus on can bring a sense of peace and can teach us that it is not our environment that makes us feel how we feel, it is what we choose to attach our attention and energy to.

Where we attach our attention
is where our energy goes

We live in a world, in a life, in a situation where there are multiple things happening at any moment. We have experienced so many different things in our past that have triggered so many different emotions. We need to become aware of which of the things in our external world or which things or events in our past we are choosing to attach our attention and focus to.

We can become excellent at attaching our attention to the things that justify our inner fears or beliefs. If we believe that we are not good enough, not fit enough, not clever enough, not deserving enough, then we will attach all our energy to the things in our environment and in our life that confirm these beliefs – and by attaching all our energy to these we completely ignore and dismiss all the other things that might actually prove these things wrong.

We can start a day with a list of ten things to do, and even if we get nine done, at night time our energy and our attention is attached to the one thing we didn't get done. Instead of falling asleep feeling proud of ourselves for having completed nine things, we fall asleep angry or feeling that we have failed because of the one we didn't get done.

When we start to become aware of where exactly we are allowing our energy to go and to what we are attaching our thoughts and energy, we can begin to make a decision on which part of our environment, which part of our day, and even which part of our past we choose to focus on.

When we choose to focus on and bring our attention and

energy to something from our past, be it earlier that day, earlier that week or even earlier in our life, it then begins to replay in our minds. If we think of something in the past, it triggers the same thoughts and emotions, it triggers the same neuro-circuitry, and by doing this we are now igniting the same parts of the brain that were ignited when the event happened for real.

We are now not just remembering but we are reliving, we are making that event, that memory, re-present itself, and our bodies and our brains cannot distinguish between a memory and an actual experience.

We know that by reliving this we are emotionally, physically, physiologically, bio-chemically and cognitively back in the same place. We are trapped in a repeating and self-perpetuating state of being imprisoned in the same reality. Regardless of what the external reality actually is, we will only attach our energy to the things that confirm and trap us in this subconscious bias.

'Having the ability to identify where you want to focus your energy and which things you will detach from is a really powerful way of claiming back your inner power and taking back your ability to manifest the life you dream of having and the person you dream of becoming.'

It is so important when we look back at our past that we identify which past we are choosing to focus on, think about and give our energy to. When we look at our external environment, it is important that we ask ourselves which things we will choose to focus on. And when we start to choose the things that make us feel safe and grounded, then we become the person who is not defined by their environment, not controlled by the environment – we become the person who is controlling their environment.

Having the ability to identify where you want to focus your energy and which things you will detach from is a really powerful way of claiming back your inner power and taking back your ability to manifest the life you dream of having and the person you dream of becoming.

18

We let go the hand of the divine

One of the biggest mistakes we make in our journey through life is that, at times, we let go of the hand of the divine. From all my explorations, from the most modern discoveries and principles in astrophysics, to the ancient teachings of the mystics, we now realise that it is no longer credible to think that this universe created itself or that it sustains itself.

We have created an unnecessary split between religion and science. We think that they are opposite beliefs and that they contradict each other. But the truth is that, very often, they actually affirm each other. Very often, they are describing the same reality using different languages, and we get caught up in the language aspect and think they are saying two different things.

Let's take a closer look.

The complexity of our created universe requires such incredible and precise balance and order for it to function as it does, and science is now shining a light into just how incredible this balance is. And the probability of it staying in such a finely tuned balance is so mind bogglingly small that we really need to accept it is not likely to happen by chance. We have to look for a scientific understanding as to how this can be.

Thermodynamics is a fundamental scientific field. The key principles or laws of thermodynamics describe the relationships between thermal energy, or heat, and other forms of energy, and how energy affects matter, which makes it a great way of examining our universe as we know our universe is a system of constant interaction of energy, heat and matter.

The fundamental laws of thermodynamics reveal two incredible facts.

The First Law of Thermodynamics states that energy cannot be created or destroyed – this means the total *quantity* of energy in the universe stays the same.

We also know from quantum physics that everything in this universe, including us humans, is fundamentally made up of energy. We know that without this presence of energy, nothing could exist. This then raises the question of how energy came about if energy cannot be created. It seems like a difficult question that leads you to a dead end but, in fact, it's an easier question to answer than you may think.

Everything we know in our universe is of the created world, the energy in our world is a created energy. Now science tells us that energy cannot create itself, which leaves science with a very simple answer. If we know that energy cannot create itself and we also know energy exists, then science has no choice but to accept that something other than the energy we know, something other than the created world, something other than the universe, created it.

Now, if we know from thermodynamics that energy cannot be destroyed or created, then we also have to apply this to us humans and our personalities. Our energy self, our soul, cannot be destroyed, only moved from one form to another and from one place to another. The very fact that it cannot be created will help us to realise that we don't have a starting point either, we have always existed in various forms, and this is very close to the mystics who have told us for thousands of years that the soul is immortal and doesn't die, it gets moved or recreated into a new form.

The Second Law of Thermodynamics is about the quality of energy. It states that as energy is transferred or transformed, more and more of it is wasted. The Second Law also states that there is a natural tendency for any isolated system to degenerate into a more disordered state. In other words, thermodynamics states that when disorder is introduced into a system, then the disorder has to increase until it eventually takes over. Let's see what this looks like in a real-life situation.

The human body obeys the laws of thermodynamics. As the sweat absorbs more and more heat, it evaporates from your body, becoming more disordered and transferring heat into the air, which heats up the air temperature of the room even more. A crowded room with closed windows and doors is a 'closed system'. Many sweating people in this closed system will quickly heat up indefinitely as there is no external thing or source to add cool air to the room. In order for the room to return to room temperature, it would need air from an outside source to come in and rebalance the temperature. The universe requires an external energy source to keep its order in balance and to keep the disorder from taking over. This external energy source has to be different from the universe itself.

This Second Law of Thermodynamics, the law of entropy, reveals that in order for this world, this universe, to remain so finely tuned, there must be an external source that is not allowing the disorder that is in the world to become the dominant force.

We know that in our universe we have natural disorders, but on the whole – from the speed at which the Earth rotates, to the magnetic forces in the universe, to the movement of the tides, the passing of the seasons – we know that the world is an ordered, electrical field, and science itself is telling us this is because there is an external energy field that is outside our known universe.

These two points of thermodynamics open up a really incredible conclusion that this universe was most likely intelligently designed, begun and is being maintained by an energy force that is different and outside of this known universe.

The word 'divine' for me simply means an energy source that is outside of our created world and an energy source that has both created and continues to sustain our universe.

> 'The word "divine" for me simply means an energy source that is outside of our created world and an energy source that has both created and continues to sustain our universe.'

While the language may be different to the mystics, here we have a very real example of where science and religion meet in harmony. What that external energy source is can be debated and disagreed upon, but the fact that there must be an external energy source outside of this universe is accepted by both science and religion.

The dichotomy between science and religion is not at all as big as people believe it is. In fact, while the language of religion and science may differ, the technical understanding of this universe and how it was created and how it is sustained in a fine-tuned perfection, in its mystifying, ever-expanding, ever-evolving manner, is where science and religion are now meeting. Every true scientist realises that there are deeper questions of life, of consciousness and of the universe that science can't fully address.

From the work of Einstein (who said the whole universe is energy and vibration and that everything that exists came from a source energy field that connects everything at all times) to the incredible work of Stephen Hawking (who pushed our understanding of astrophysics to a whole new level) to the work of Deepak Chopra, when we distil the points at which they arrived after a lifetime of study and research, we realise that all these incredible minds are often saying the same thing using different language: everything in this universe, including humans, is energy.

Energy cannot be created so it doesn't have a beginning and it can't be destroyed, so it has no end. It is eternal, and in order for the universe, which is a closed system, to remain balanced the way it is, there must be an external source outside of this universe correcting and guiding us. It's mind-blowing.

Where the problem arises for humans is when we let go the hand of the divine and the understanding of the divine. We stop believing that something has created and sustains this universe. We begin to believe that this universe, that is so finely tuned, is simply a random act of randomness. We ignore the findings of both science and religion, and we choose to believe that the universe is a creation that is simply set up to serve us humans. Despite the Earth playing such a tiny role in the universe, we somehow begin to believe that the Earth is the most important planet in the universe. We must remember that there are at least 200 billion stars in our own galaxy, and there are maybe 400 billion galaxies in our observable universe, each one of them with billions of stars.

We also tell ourselves lies, such as that humans are the most enlightened of all species. Yet, the facts show that the humans are the species that struggle the most, humans are the ones causing the most damage to themselves and to this planet. We must also remember that the only ones saying that humans are the most enlightened species are humans. No one else and nothing else either says it or points to it. In fact, all the evidence is in favour of the opposite. We are the last to arrive, the ones still struggling to find our place and the ones with the most amount of anxiety and self-doubt.

I believe this is because we have forgotten that we are just a part of this incredible masterpiece. We have forgotten that we are not mechanical robots walking around in nature. We have forgotten that we are nature and that everything we do has an impact on nature. We have forgotten that everything we do to nature, we are actually doing to ourselves.

There is no escaping the fact that everything in this created universe is connected and finely balanced and yet we don't live in a way that honours this sensitive connection between all things.

We have forgotten that we are walking, talking energy fields and that, as energy fields, we share and are connected to the same energy fields as the entire universe. This disbelief in our connection to the universe makes us think, act and live in ways that abandon our spiritual and energy connection to the universe.

When we abandon our spiritual connection, we let go the hand of the divine. Our fragile human sense of self, our fragile human ego, becomes terrified, terrified that we are not enough, not good enough, not big enough, not important enough. In this terrified illusion of insignificance, our ego takes over and we spend our lives trying to prove that we are enough. But the truth is we can never be enough, or we can never feel enough, if we are disconnected from our spiritual energy field, our true source.

We can and will never feel big enough or good enough if we don't realise that we are not mechanical robots in the universe but that we are the universe connected to all things at all times and that all of the beautiful mystery of the universe is in each and every one of us. I believe this human fear of not being big enough or good enough is what drives most of the human suffering on this planet.

Imagine a jigsaw piece that removes itself from the rest of the jigsaw. It spends the rest of its life as a single disconnected piece. Without the rest of the pieces, the one jigsaw piece can never be what it is meant to be. It can never reflect the full, beautiful picture that it is meant to reflect, and without the other pieces to fit into, the shape of the single jigsaw piece will never make any sense to itself. The jigsaw piece will only make sense, will only feel at home, will only reflect its true picture, when it is connected to all the other pieces. We humans are like the disconnected jigsaw piece. We have removed ourselves from the masterpiece of the universe and because we are now disconnected nothing makes any sense to us. We don't even make sense to ourselves. We feel alone and afraid, afraid that we are not enough, not good enough, not important enough, not loved enough.

This drives most wars. It drives the need for certain communities to stockpile food and money, while half of our planet struggles for food. How can we live in a world that has more food and money than it needs and yet one of the biggest killers of human beings is malnutrition and starvation?

There is a fear that is rampant in the human race, a fear driven by a sense and a feeling of disconnection, and the only way we can eliminate this fear is by realising and remembering that we are a small but powerful part of the overall masterpiece that is the universe. But that we are only powerful when we are connected in a spiritual way, as energy fields, to all that exists. By surrendering the human ego and the human need to understand and control everything, we can then replace this need to control with a simple need to be. To be part of, to be connected to, to hold the hand of the divine.

The word 'divine' can mean many things to many people. Different religions might differ on their version of the divine. Science and religion may differ on their definition of the divine, but we need to remember there is a divine, an external, universal energy source. Regardless of how we label it, there is an energy field, a powerful external source that both created and sustains this universe.

This energy field had the ability and imagination to create this incredible universe and it also created you. With the same care, love and precision that created the universe, you were created. You are not a mistake; you are an incredible and special part of the divine masterpiece. You are not here to apologise or to play small. You are not here to think that you're an independent mechanical robot looking at an energy field that we call the universe, you *are* the universe. You are the same energy field that sustains all of the universe.

When we realise and ignite our energy fields, when we deeply and truly become connected to everything that is and we trust in the universe with all our hearts, we replace fear with trust and anger with love, and we become more powerful than we could ever imagine.

It is time that we brought the findings of science and religion together. It is time that we brought the disciplines of medicine, neuroscience, psychology, astrophysics and quantum physics together. We can never discover the true meaning and nature of this universe while any of these fields is disregarded.

We can never fully realise who we truly are until we unlock and open our minds to the discoveries of these fields. We need to start connecting the dots to which they're all pointing.

When we open our eyes and open all minds to the unquestionable and incredible mystery of this universe, we can then start to truly nourish ourselves in the mystery and awe of ourselves and this universe. We can release ourselves from the struggle of having to understand and control and, with humility, ease and grace, wake up and commit to living a life that is more connected, more grounded and more spiritually aware than ever before.

The world is waking up to the spiritual reality that is part of each and every person. When we waken to our spiritual self, we begin to realise how powerful and incredible it all is and how powerful the force that designed and created it must be. The gift of connection, the gift of feeling complete and the gift of feeling good enough floods through our systems the moment we reach out and we hold the hand of the divine in unconditional faith and trust.

19

It's up to you

You cannot outrun the things that are in your head and in your heart

Health and wellness have nothing to do with diets, starvation of the body or starvation of the soul, they have nothing to do with deprivation or constantly pushing yourself to the limit. These things are more to do with inner fear, anger, guilt or shame and even self-punishment.

While food and exercise are an important part of wellness, so is balance. We can't engage in diets or exercise routines that are simply another, albeit socially acceptable, way of expressing an internal destructive emotion. If we find that we have a tendency to be emotionally angry or fearful, then developing an exercise or eating pattern that enables and increases these negative emotions is simply adding to our ill-health.

A healthy body in the absence of a healthy mind and a healthy spirit is like painting a wall when the bricks of the wall are crumbling. Exercise regimes that constantly push us to our limit are often expressions of inner anger and an inner belief that we need to be punished. Diets and nutritional plans that deprive us and teach us that food is the enemy are often based on inner fear or a feeling that our body needs or deserves to be deprived or starved. We can take diet and exercise to an unhealthy extreme.

Sometimes, we need to climb big, scary mountains and feel the exhilaration of that achievement. Sometimes, we need to be still and silent and admire their beauty from afar. There are not enough mountains or triathlons on this planet to satisfy an angry human spirit that's terrified of standing still. We will eventually run out of external things to conquer, and if we haven't actually conquered ourselves, then all the mountains and triathlons may mean very little.

You cannot outrun the things that are in your head and in your heart. Compassion is the ultimate green juice and love is the ultimate superfood.

Our world does not need more training plans or more fitness regimes where we get fit, get in shape and then stop and get unfit and out of shape again and end up where we started because we didn't really address the root cause of why we were out of shape.

Real healing and health is not about more drive or determination, it's about compassion and forgiveness. Our inner world especially needs it. Our external world is a reflection of our internal world and our external

> 'You cannot outrun the things that are in your head and in your heart. Compassion is the ultimate green juice and love is the ultimate superfood.'

relationships become reflections of the relationship we have with our inner self. When we can love and forgive ourselves, we can love and forgive others.

The hardest realisation we all need to make is that we are the common denominator – if we don't change, nothing changes.

The hardest thing for me first and foremost is when I meet a client for the first time. I go into a business where I meet the team leader who wants me to work with their team because they think the team lacks focus and the ability to be present and execute well under pressure.

I observe the team and the people on the team for a while and then I go back to the leader to give them my opinion about the source and the possible resolution of the problem. When I meet the leader, they are usually tight on time and rushing. They are also talking a hundred miles an hour and they're breathing shallowly and quickly. They are very often drinking coffee and, while I am observing this, they are asking me what the problem with the team or the business is.

I might be sitting with the CEO, I'm observing all of their heightened anxiety, their constant state of distraction and of course I have to break the bad news to them.

They ask, 'Do you see the problem, Gerry?'

'Yes,' I answer, 'I see the problem. I see it clearly.'

They will then start to predict where the problem is and they will go all around the business from area to area because, of course, they think the problem is somewhere else in the business; they are frantically looking out and not for a second looking inward.

The conversation will go something like this: 'Is it the HR department?'

'No, it's not HR.'

'Is it the legal department?'

'No, it's not the legal team.'

They will keep going around every external place where the problem may be, without ever coming even close to the real source. Eventually, they start getting annoyed and ask, 'Well, where is the problem?'

It's at that point that I have to be brave and tell the truth. I ask them, 'Do you really want me to tell you? Do you really want me to tell you where the problem is?'

They'll tell me that they do and then I tell them the hard but honest part: 'It's you.'

Most of us have to realise that we are at least 50 per cent of our own environment. The hardest part for me is to sit in front of a client and tell them that they are the problem – it's their response, their state of mind and their state of being that is the problem.

WHAT WE DON'T REPAIR, WE REPEAT

The secret is you. The starting point is you and the first thing that needs to change is you. If you don't change on the inside, then nothing on the outside will ever change. We simply repeat what we don't repair.

The hardest but most important questions we all need to ask ourselves are: How am I contributing to my own chaos? How am I contributing to my own problem? What if I was to focus on this and change it?

The hardest thing at times is to look in the mirror, but when we realise that often our problem is looking back at us, we get to realise that great empowering and freeing reality: if our problem is in the mirror, then so too is our solution.

The secret to everything, the secret to becoming your true self, of overcoming what is holding you back in life, is staring you right in the face every time you look in the mirror, and the secret to everything you ever wanted is also staring you in the face every time you look in the mirror.

We must also be careful that we take responsibility and accountability, that we are not using this as a stick to further beat ourselves up with. Taking personal ownership and accountability is about moving forward in a healthy and compassionate way and has nothing to do with blaming or giving out to yourself.

Don't outsource your health, wellness or happiness

Very often when we are not observing our own inner world, our actions or the decisions we are making, we can often outsource our own freedom, our own power and even our health. We begin to believe that the answer to everything we need is outside us. We begin to doubt ourselves and our own inner intelligence, we can often then need to seek validation from external sources.

THE MOST TRUTHFUL QUESTIONS ARE THE ONES
THAT BRING THE GREATEST OPPORTUNITIES

Some really important questions are:

- Do you know who you are, and how much do you love that person you are?
- When you look in the mirror are you deeply proud of the person you see looking back?
- If you truly loved yourself and realised how short life is, what changes would you make?
- If you aren't already making these changes, what is holding you back?
- What are the beliefs you hold about yourself that are keeping you in the place you are?
- What are the beliefs you hold about yourself that are keeping you in a job you don't like/a relationship that doesn't make you happy?

When we were in the womb, we all somehow had the ability to create and shape ourselves. The sad point is that most of us go from having this incredible ability to create ourselves using our inner wisdom to a point where we can't seem to make any decisions about what we should do.

We need external people to tell us what to eat, how to exercise, not to drink excessively, we even need external devices to tell us we need to sleep and that we need to move. We surrender all our inner power to external people or external sources, and we begin to outsource our own happiness and our own dreams.

Very often, people will tell me that the doctor has them on antibiotics, they will say this believing that this is the truth. Then, I ask them if it is the doctor that has them on antibiotics or if it is their lifestyle. The truth often is their lifestyle but that is the very thing they are overlooking and they are outsourcing their health to a doctor. No matter how powerful an external health professional is, they are only part of the healing.

We actively contribute to and create the lives and situations we live in

We are often like 3D printers. We externally project and manifest the things we think about and the emotions we hold. Our world will not be healed by constant external transformation; it will be healed by returning to our source, by reconnecting with our inner spark and reigniting our human spirit.

Our world is craving simplicity and love. The thoughts we think and the inner stories we use are constantly reshaping our very beliefs and programmes. These thoughts are constantly sending a vibrational frequency into the universe and helping shape our very experience of the outside world. And this brings us back to the Eliot poem I mentioned at the beginning of the book, titled 'Four Quartets':

And the end of all our exploring
Will be to arrive where we started
And know the place for the first time.

All of life, by the decisions you make, the things you prioritise and the things you focus on, is either an incredible, enlightening journey back to your real self, a journey that liberates you and sets your free, or it is a journey of moving further away from your true self, a journey where you get distracted by things that don't actually matter, a journey where you settle for social affirmation and surrender self-expression, a journey where you become what you think others want you to be and you sacrifice the person you think you could be.

All of life is a journey back to our beginning, back to who we truly are, back to who we were in our truest, purest form but this time having learned, let go of or given away that which we were sent here to do.

All of life, everything that happens to us, all of the people and situations we encounter, are simply ways for us to discover the true depth of who we are and the incredible and often infinite amount of love, kindness, forgiveness that we all have within our heart.

But do you have faith?

The opposite of faith is fear. In a world where some say there are only two human emotions, love and fear, I say there is only one human emotion and that is love. Everything else is the absence of love. Fear is not the opposite of love, it is the absence of love.

Faith is love, faith is a full and unconditional love where there is no doubt. Doubt is just another name for fear.

In this life, we need love, unconditional love, and therefore we need faith. It can be faith in many things – faith in our world, faith in our loved ones, faith in ourselves and possibly faith in an existential being or energy source.

Most people, when it comes to it, do not have sufficient faith; especially when it comes to themselves, most people do not have faith in themselves.

Three very simple questions to check the faith you have in yourself are:

- Do you believe you are capable of achieving everything you dream of?
- Do you believe you deserve everything that you dream of?
- Do you believe you are deserving of all love?

Until we can answer yes to all three of these questions, we will be trapped in a faithless, self-created existence, a self-limited absence of faith. Without that faith to propel us forwards, we will get stuck, stuck in the safety of the known and stuck in the limits of your familiar past.

Until you begin to see yourself through the eyes of the people who love you, until you begin to see yourself as the infinite loving being that you are, until you begin to recognise that you are a special part of this incredible universe, that you are not a mistake and you are not here to play small, until you believe that – really believe it with all your heart – then you will be trapped in a life where the only thing you fulfil is your own self-doubt.

We don't get to live once, we die once – we get to live every day

There is an expression that says you only live once. I have never agreed with it – in fact, I think it is completely misleading. My belief is that we only die once and we get to live every single day. My belief is that every day is a lifetime and every lifetime is a day.

We know that our body is constantly renewing itself on a daily basis. We know that the more we nourish our mind and emotions, we are also changing on a cognitive and emotional level also. The truth is that we are not physically the same person that we were ten years ago, five years ago or even one year ago.

As long as we choose to change and upgrade our thoughts and emotions on a regular basis, then no part of us is the same as it was in our past, and the things that happened to us in the past did not actually happen to this person we are today.

There comes a point when we need to make a decision to refresh and renew our inner thinking and beliefs, to let go of the old and remember that we are renewed on a daily basis.

Each day is a day we have never lived before. It is a day we will never live again. The only question is: Are you choosing to live each new day in a new way?

Do you embrace each new day as this new physical, mental and emotional being or are you infecting each new day with the same thinking and emotions of the past? We can infect the biology of the present with the thoughts and emotions of the past, each day is just another day of the same where our present and our future looks and feels exactly like the past. Every cell in your body is changing all the time. When we choose to release our self from the thinking and the emotions of the past, we realise that, each and every day, we get an opportunity to start again as somebody new. We get an opportunity to live each and every day as a truly unique experience.

At the end of the day, we get to release the parts of ourselves that no longer serve us. Each and every night, we get to release and let go of the old and, each morning, we get to begin again, reborn and renewed.

Never allow what's in your head to stop you going after what's in your heart

In our short 900 months, we get one chance – this is not a dress rehearsal. Deep in your heart, you know who you can be, you know what you dream of and you know that you deserve the life you dream of. The only questions you need to answer are: Do you love yourself enough to give it a go? Do you love yourself enough to not worry about what others think?

Do you love yourself enough to let go of your past and embrace the new? Who you were, up to this minute? What you have done?

Who you have been up to this minute has absolutely nothing to do with who you can be in the future and what you can have.

The only question is: Do you love yourself enough to go after it?

My biggest discovery, the one thing that I am absolutely certain of, is that, regardless of the situation, regardless of the question, the answer is always another question: What would love do?

If you truly loved yourself, if you truly loved yourself and knew you had 600 months to live, what would you do? Say it, say it out loud, say it with all your heart and all your soul.

Now go take the first step. Then, go do it with all your heart and all your soul and make sure at the end of your 900 months you have no regrets.

20

A practical guide to implementing the learnings and insights from this book into your everyday life

Our life is not changed by what we know but what we do

The process of inner change requires inner work. It is not enough to read, you have to practise what you read, and this needs time and effort.

There is no such thing as instant self-improvement. Any inner change takes time, and there must be motivation, desire, ambition, perseverance and dedication. Outer and inner resistance and opposition must be taken into account too.

When starting any self-improvement programme, most people usually encounter inner resistance that comes from their old habits and their subconscious mind, and also resistance and opposition from the people around them. The desire to change, build new habits and improve must be strong enough to resist any laziness, desire to give up, and ridicule or opposition from family, friends or colleagues.

Before beginning this process, we must accept that there will be challenges and resistance. We must accept that it will take time and that, like all journeys, this will be taken one step at a time.

A practical guide to starting your day

Having a morning routine is a really important way to wake up and greet your new day. It can automatically reduce stress, as it eliminates that morning 'rush', which inevitably leads to a 'grab and go' breakfast and sends out a chaotic signal into your energetic field, almost like you're chasing a wild horse for the day yet you never catch the horse!

Having a morning ritual gives you structure, creates a sense of self-care and self-nourishment, and brings calmness and balance into your life.

The energy you wake up in, the emotions you feel and the mental thoughts you meet the day with have great power and potential to dictate how your day will go. You either attack your day with vengeance and anger or you greet your day with openness and gratitude.

'The energy you wake up in, the emotions you feel and the mental thoughts you meet the day with have great power and potential to dictate how your day will go. You either attack your day with vengeance and anger or you greet your day with openness and gratitude.'

Creating a peaceful morning ritual helps to create a peaceful day that, in turn, results in a more peaceful life.

Morning routines for well-being

1. Morning reflective pages

The secret to a great day can actually be a very simple morning practice suggested by Julia Cameron in her famous book *The Artists' Way*. Every morning, take a pen and some blank pages and write down whatever you feel needs to be released. This practice is called 'Morning Pages' and it acts as a mind dump to get rid of clutter from your brain. It's simply a conscious stream of writing from mind to pen, and pen to paper.

There is no wrong way to do Morning Pages. It is simply about anything and everything that crosses your mind, and is for your eyes only. Do not over-think things, just write things down on three pages on the first day, and then do three more pages the next day, and so on.

This ritual helps to reduce the feelings of being overwhelmed or panicked. This practice will enable, clarify, comfort, cajole, prioritise and synchronise the day at hand.

It sets you up for a calmer, clearer and more productive day.

2. Visualisation

The daily practice of visualising your dreams as already having been completed has huge power to rapidly accelerate your achievement of those dreams, goals and ambitions.

On waking, take a few brief moments to visualise how you want your day to go. Visualise how you look, how you walk, how you feel. Visualise yourself smiling, laughing or singing. By visualising what you want, and focusing on what you have as opposed to what you don't have, you will greatly dictate how your day will run. By developing a morning ritual of visualising a healthy and happy image, you will begin to create a happy and healthy life.

3. Gratitude/Prayer

Practise a few minutes of daily gratitude to contemplate the blessings you have in your life. For example, 'Today I am blessed to see the sun rise', 'Today I am blessed to smell my cup of morning coffee', 'Today I am blessed to have a warm shower'.

Write down everything that your body provides that you are grateful for in this moment. Take time to thank you and your body. Place your hands on your heart and really thank it. Life is miraculous. You are a miracle.

4. Exercise and movement

Movement is vital to help release emotions out of the body (remember the word emotion means 'e-motive', energy in motion). It also produces endorphins, which are your body's natural internal morphine. In addition, movement helps reduce pain, and releases tension and stress, both physically and emotionally.

5. Breathing

Take five deep belly breaths. Set triggers to remind yourself – for example, take five deep breaths before starting your car, before opening your laptop, while waiting for the kettle to boil, while waiting at traffic lights, etc. This is a powerful way to reduce stress and anxiety.

6. Positive affirmations

The things you say are being listened to all the time by your subconscious mind and they are forming your beliefs. By regularly using self- and life-affirming sentences and phrases you are creating a new inner language and new inner beliefs.

7. Self-talk – listen, check and reframe

The stories we tell ourselves, the thoughts we think and the pictures we create in our minds are the biggest dictators of the life we lead.

You create your own reality by the thoughts you think and the words you say. Choose your words carefully. Consciously say something nice to yourself or a loved one first thing in the morning. Remember: energy flows where your thoughts go.

Changing your story will change your day. Changing your days will change your life. Each morning brings about a new day. A day in which you have never ever lived before. Each and every day has infinite possibilities and opportunities, so tell yourself stories that expand and open your heart and mind to the opportunities and potential in this incredible world and in you. You have the power to change your day in small ways, thereby transforming the way you feel.

8. Meditation

Take a mindful pause and become the observer of your thoughts. Check in with yourself to see how you are feeling/doing. Notice your thoughts. Are they opening or closing your heart? Are they enabling you to have a day that is more aligned with a calm and relaxed state or are they taking you into a more frightened, stressful state? Take a deep breath and refocus. Continue to take a few deep belly breaths. Reset and restart your day from this place of inner calm and ease.

Night-time routines for well-being

1. Go tech-free for one to two hours before bed

Screens emit blue light that stimulates the brain, and the light tells the brain to stay awake. Melatonin is the sleep-inducing hormone, and our bodies won't produce this unless we are exposed to darker light. Blue light equals a sleepless night.

2. Make sure your room is dark

This will enable melatonin to be produced in the pineal gland and assist with sleep.

3. No tech in the bedroom

So, ideally, no TV, radios, laptops, phones in the bedroom.

4. Have your last meal two to three hours before bed

If your body and brain is occupied with digesting your food, it will take away from your ability to sleep.

5. Aromatherapy

Try using aromatherapy to help you get a good night's sleep; calming, sleep-inducing aromas like lavender, rose or jasmine can help.

6. Mindful preparation

Taking a warm bath or shower before bed can also help with getting a good night's sleep. It can be used as a good mental, emotional or physical trigger to cleanse away the day. Let it wash away any unwanted thoughts, feelings or emotions.

7. Relax

Listening to a night-time meditation or engaging in some deep breathing is a great way to help the mind switch off and enable the body to relax.

SELF-CARE PRACTICES

As my wife Miriam says, 'Self-care is not a delicacy, it's a necessity.'

Can you give yourself the permission to take fifteen minutes (just over 1 per cent of your entire day) to nurture and care for yourself? To commit to developing a self-care regimen and developing a loving, harmonious relationship with yourself, choose from this list of tools/practices to help:

Compassionate self-talk
Regularly throughout your day, pause to notice your inner dialogue. How are you speaking to yourself? What's the tone you are using? Is it kind and compassionate or is it laced with judgement, resentment or comparison? Can you begin to show more compassion towards yourself through the words and stories you use when speaking to yourself about yourself? Try speaking to yourself like you would speak to a loved one. Remember that your inner self is always listening. Start today.

Me-time moments
This can be anything that just gives you a few moments to unplug from the external world and drop into a space of calm. This might be anything from running yourself a hot bath, to getting on your yoga mat for ten minutes. It might be baking, painting, drawing, gardening or even taking a

little nap. When you come back to your day, the likelihood is that you will be more refreshed, more centred and have more joy in your heart.

Nature and the great outdoors
Natural healing therapy takes place when you spend time in the outdoors. Make time to get fresh air every day. Get out of the office and walk around the block on your lunch break. Oxygenate the cells and this will help re-energise your mind and body.

The power of the breath
Your breath is extremely powerful when used correctly and has regular healing effects. It is one of the best ways to reduce stress, heart rate, blood pressure and overall anxiety and fear, and bring you back into the present moment.

Take the time to stop and breathe in through your nose. Send the breath to your belly, letting it rise. Pause at the top of your inhale and then breathe out slowly through your mouth. Let your belly fall as you breathe out. Repeat this regularly throughout the day for greater well-being.

Meditation, mindfulness, prayer and gratitude
All of these are powerful tools to help gain more clarity, focus and calmness in your life.

Open communication

Talk it out, cry it out – release the emotion through communicating with a trusted person or a trained professional.

Unplugging

Unplug from the busyness of the world. Refrain from the urgency to 'do' and try to just 'be'. Connecting with yourself and others on a real human level, heart to heart, is where real healing and happiness occurs. Set aside time during dinner where all phones are put away, or have a 'no phone or technology in the bedroom' rule. Try choosing a day, or an hour each day, where you will detach from texting, checking social media and responding to emails. You will begin to experience a richer life.

The importance of connection

Studies have found that oxytocin levels (our love and connection hormone) have been greatly reduced because of the increase in our use of technology. Oxytocin soars when we feel connected. Human beings are social creatures built to thrive on human connection and community. However, as we break away from the tribe and become more at one with our screens than with other human beings, our oxytocin levels drop and we feel a sense of isolation and loneliness, often developing a lack of trust and a sense of danger.

Oxytocin levels are raised by giving and receiving hugs, touch, massage and intimacy. Cuddle your dog, your kids, your partner, your teddy or book a massage! Place your hands on your heart and say thank you each morning – all of these are powerful yet incredibly simple ways to waken your own inner pharmacy. Giving and receiving love is one of the most powerful tools for enhancing health and well-being. To help raise your oxytocin levels, try meeting up with friends more regularly and having real face-to-face contact and conversations. Join a local society or gym, or volunteer with a charity.

Rest, recovery and reflection
We must build regular periods into our day and our week where we take time to stop, to breathe and to reflect.

Ask for help
Allow yourself to be real and human and vulnerable. A problem shared is a problem halved.

Food and nutrition
Eat wholesome, real food, reduce processed, chemically artificial, packaged products. Reduce stimulants such as sugar, coffee and alcohol, as they increase nervous tension and anxiety.

Practical guide to building inner confidence

Start your day by affirming and building your self-confidence. Here are some tips:

Acknowledge yourself

Too often in life, we place our focus on the future. If we are constantly planning for the future, then we can often neglect the present. It is so important for the soul that we praise ourselves on a regular basis and reaffirm to ourselves that we are genuinely making progress. However small our accomplishments, we should acknowledge them to ourselves and take the opportunity to see the goodness we are creating.

Remind yourself of your strengths and achievements

One way is to make a list of things you like about yourself. Or keep a 'success' file of awards, certificates and positive letters or citations. Keep mementos of accomplishments you are proud of where you can see them. End each day by listing your wins from the day; however big or small they are, they are all important.

Forgive yourself when you don't do all you hoped

Building internal self-esteem and self-nurturing can be surprisingly hard if you are not used to doing it. Try to imagine that you are another individual. Put all the facts about yourself on the table and think about whether this other person would forgive you for whatever mistakes you made. Very often we realise that we judge ourselves far more harshly than others judge us.

Remember not to focus merely on the result or outcome. Every action should be considered from a wider perspective, taking into account our intentions, our expectations, our knowledge at the time of the incident and our willingness to move on from it. Remember that when you hold a hurt inside, it gets worse and, eventually, leaks into the whole personality. Forgiving yourself is a liberating experience that frees the soul and not only brings happiness into your own life but the lives of the people you meet.

Get physical

Practise specific yoga poses, including power poses and mudras (a Sanskrit word for sacred and symbolic hand and finger postures) that focus on activating the solar plexus – the third energy centre in the body that is related to igniting inner belief, passion, courage and confidence.

Look after your mental and emotional fitness

Begin to develop your confidence and belief in yourself by working on developing greater mental fitness and strengthening your emotional immune system. Simple ways to help this include practising routines and rituals like visualisation, positive affirmations, journalling, gratitude, meditation, deep breathing, talk therapy and energy medicine.

CODE – Turn knowledge into action

The next section will highlight the practical application of our learnings from this book and how we translate them into our CODE – our Calendar of Daily Events. It's a simple and powerful way of ensuring that we are living what we know about health and wellness in really practical and powerful ways, not just now and again but every day.

Our life is not determined by what we do now and again, it's determined by what we do every day, the habits and routines that we embed into our everyday lives.

I have included a menu of sample items. Of course, you are not expected to do them all but I want to provide a choice so that you can pick the ones that best suit you and also so that you can have variety and choice to keep your daily practices fresh and innovative. Use the following chart as a daily template. Each morning, circle or tick the activities you would like to do that day and at night, circle or tick which ones you implemented that day.

Body routines	Mind routines	Soul routines
Wholesome, nutritious food	Morning intentions	Prayer/Meditation
Stretch/Yoga	Gratitude	Conscious breathing
Home-cooked food	Positive affirmations	Meaningful connections
Physical activity	Reading/Painting/Drawing	Loving work
Mindful eating	Journalling/Writing/Morning Pages	Laughter/Play
Hydration	Visualising my future	Listening to music/Singing
Quality sleep		Time in nature
Fresh air		
Touch/Massage		

Summary

Understanding the human condition

We are:
- electrical energy fields; energy cannot be destroyed, it can only be moved
- not robots or mechanical machines walking around in nature, we *are* nature and we are connected to everything that exists
- social beings who crave to love and to be loved
- infinite spiritual beings.

We are born with:
- incredible inner resilience
- an infinite inner ability to learn
- an inner need to love and be loved
- a fully integrated mind, body and spirit
- an open heart
- an absorbent and adaptive brain
- an infinite spirit
- zero self-criticism
- a blank inner dialogue.

We come to:

- learn a lesson, awaken our consciousness and release the thing that is keeping us from peace
- bring light for others
- be an important part of the incredible jigsaw of the universe
- help others to find their own inner light and release their fears
- find peace.

We seek:

- union with ourselves
- union with the divine
- release from the past
- meaning.

We thrive when we feel:

- connected
- respected
- trusted
- valued
- loved.

We learn to:

- adapt
- fear
- compare
- judge
- self-criticise.

We develop:
- a belief about the world in which we live
- a belief about ourselves, in which we live
- an ego
- coping mechanisms, healthy and unhealthy
- inner stories that suit our inner beliefs
- internal and external reward and recognition patterns
- unconscious bias and expectations
- internal voices.

We take on:
- other people's voices
- other people's beliefs about the world
- other people's beliefs about ourselves
- roles that serve our emotional needs.

We live:
- within our beliefs
- in ways that pursue love or avoid pain
- in ways that give us instant gratification
- within the limits of the physical.

We become imprisoned by:
- our subconscious programmes and beliefs
- our inner thoughts and stories
- our inner critic
- our ego
- the roles we play

- the people we surround ourselves with
- our past
- other people's expectations.

We lose:
- our connection to the divine
- sight of our own inner divine
- experience of inner peace
- courage to speak our truths
- courage to pursue our dreams
- our inner fearless child.

We are liberated by:
- self-compassion
- self-acceptance
- spiritual awakening
- subconscious reprogramming.

Acknowledgements

Miriam, you are the centre of my universe, the source of my inspiration, and it is with you that I am at home. Thank you for not just allowing me to explore the infinite but for being the reason I believe in it.

Elijah, I often wondered if my life would amount to much. The moment you arrived I had my answer. You are the greatest gift, and being your dad is my greatest honour ever.

To my dad: You are my giant, my hero, and I love you with all my heart. You have given me the gift of knowing when to be strong and when to be gentle and that, often, it is our faith that gives us our greatest strength.

To my mum: You are an infinite shining light of fun, compassion and generosity. You have dared to love me when I could not love myself. Because of you, I know there are angels and they live among us. Thank you for loving me.

Thank you to Faith O'Grady. You had the immediate openness to give me and this book a chance and then the passion and belief that this could be a powerful and transformative book. I can't thank you enough for your kindness, trust and your passion to share this message. I will be forever grateful.

Ciara Doorley, you have been the steadfast and constant guide and light who has encouraged me to open my mind and soul, and you have been the patient mind that has taken my thoughts and passions and turned them into a structured sequence without ever once restricting my ideas or flow. It is a gift to work with you.

Hachette, thank you for trusting in me to write this book and for the passion and commitment you have shown me.

Finally, to you the reader. Thank you for choosing this book, thank you for opening your heart and mind to its message. I hope above all else it reminds you that you are a beautiful and powerful soul deserving of all love, peace and happiness.

Thank you from the bottom of my heart.

NOTES

NOTES

NOTES

NOTES

NOTES

NOTES

NOTES

NOTES